John Hanna is the husband of Cecil Griffiths'
granddaughter. After a varied working life including
stalking the corridors of Whitehall as a civil servant and
working on the excavation of the Mary Rose as a marine
archaeologist, he is now retired. This is his first book.

ONLY GOLD MATTERS

JOHN HANNA

Chequered Flag PUBLISHING

First published in the UK by Chequered Flag Publishing
PO Box 4669, Sheffield, S6 9ET
www.chequeredflagpublishing.co.uk

A CIP record for this book is available from the British Library

Printed in the EU by Print Group Sp. z o.o.

ISBN 9780956946058

All photographs from the author's collection unless indicated

To Cec's sons.
John inspired me to write his father's biography. Rees
inspired me to try and lead a good life. His granddaughters
– my daughters – will be the proud custodians of Cec's
legacy.

Also in memory of Lila.
She crossed my path the night of Cec's induction to the
Welsh Sports Hall of Fame.

CONTENTS

RULES FOR COMPETITION
UNDER AAA LAW 1923

Rule 1
An amateur is one who has never competed for a money prize or monetary consideration in any Athletic Sport or Game... or in any way exploited his athletic ability for profit; and who has never taken part in any athletic competition with anyone who is not an amateur.

1

GRASS
ROOTS
SEPTEMBER 1915

Cecil Redvers Bobs Griffiths – Cec to friends and family – was just fifteen years old when he took his mark for a junior running race, part of the Great September Fair in his home town of Neath, South Wales in 1915. Nearly a hundred years later, his place in history is defined by two races. This was not one of them. It was far more important.

Cec would lift many trophies and break many records, but the greatest prize in his life was won that day on the hastily marked-out grass track in front of a small crowd of people at a minor, unrecorded event. Her name was Gladys May Rees.

Cec had been named after the popular General Redvers Buller VC of Boer War fame who had built his reputation on leading men from the front. Cec was slight of stature, barely five and a half feet tall, with a gentle demeanour. He didn't exactly fit the image of a heroic leader like his namesake, but he was exquisitely proportioned with strong sinuous muscles which graced him with a breathtaking turn of speed.

Cec was in his element as he prepared for the one lap dash. The other competitors shunned him, fearing they might betray a sign of their weakness. They all knew Cec was the best. When he was at school he had played on the wing for Neath Schoolboys, the junior branch of the town's rugby club. He had been called 'the fastest thing on two legs' by his pals. If it hadn't been for the First World War, which all but shut down club rugby in Wales, he would probably have made a career in that sport, but Cec turned his sporting attention to athletics instead. The world was deprived of his considerable skills with the oval ball, but his reputation has only been enhanced by his speed on the track.

All things being equal, Cec's fellow runners were competing for the minor places, but in a handicap race, anything could happen or be made to happen. Cec was the only one to start on scratch, requiring him to cover the full race distance. He would have to run his fastest to win, overtaking all his opponents. Some had as much as 50 yards head start. Clearly Cec's reputation had preceded him.

It was a race he really wanted to win. Cec was desperate to take home the novel and valuable prize put up by his uncle, Major William Burrows Trick, commander of Neath's local defence force, the Volunteer Training Corps. He had provided silver shillings in the place of trophies. It was a thinly-veiled ploy to encourage the local men to enlist – to take the King's shilling – and fight the Hun. The travelling vans of Henry Studt at the showground on the Bird-in-Hand field in the centre of town were being used as a military recruiting office. Cec was too young to sign up, but the shillings would be a real help to a family that was tightening its belt as the German U-boat blockade began to hit.

Concentrating on the starter, Cec blocked out the happy noise of the families shouting encouragement to their sons. He believed that none of the cheers were for him – his father was dead and the rest of the family were working – but he was wrong. There was one young girl supporting him, although his occupied mind failed to register her soft voice calling out his name.

The race was being run on the Court Herbert playing fields beside the railway line, with the Neath Grammar School sports field on the other side. Modern development of this area to the north-west of the town has been minimal, so Cec would still recognise where he ran. Although Neath's location is now idyllic, nestling alongside the meandering river of the same name, in 1915 it was a town dominated by the heavy iron and steel industry fuelled by the rich seams of coal mined from deep below its verdant valley. The railway thrived on this commerce and trains ran frequently along the embankment between the two fields.

The Vale of Neath Railway had been incorporated into the Great Western Railway in 1865 and some of the old steam locomotives betrayed its heritage. Deep in concentration on the start line, Cec was distracted by the whistle of an approaching train. It passed close by, shrouded in steam and smoke. Cec was mesmerised by the motion of the steel coupling rods powering the train's massive wheels. Perhaps he envisaged himself hurtling along, arms locked at the elbows, one thrusting forward, one thrusting back, parallel with the ground for each graceful stride, hands coming to the centre of his body in perfect symmetry to mirror the dynamics of the coupling rods. Arm action is crucial to balance the body while running – Cec had the classic piston method advocated by coaches. He wasn't taught it; it just came naturally to him. Combined with his elegant long stride, his style was balanced and economical of effort, a unique method which would be his signature on the race track and the reason why seasoned observers of athletics in the future would describe him as a beautiful runner.

As the official in his white jacket raised the grey pistol above his head, the noise from the train overwhelmed him. Realising the unfortunate timing of the train's appearance, the starter held them a little too long before firing.

Cec, leaning forward over the line, was unsettled by the delay. He snatched a sideways glance through the dark, wavy hair hanging over his eyes at the elderly starter with his arm aloft holding the revolver.

The adrenaline coursing through Cec's body made him alert to the tiniest of movements. As he sensed the man's finger squeezing the trigger, his leg muscles twitched and he pushed explosively against the foot holes he had dug in the soft ground.

As Cec accelerated away for what he believed was a perfect start, he thought he heard the gun's echo. But it was not the sound bouncing off the embankment beside the track – it was a second shot, indicating there had been a false start.

Cec pictured in a school portrait of 1914

2

A NEATH

HOME
1900-1915

On his way home from the race, Cec hoped he wouldn't meet anyone he knew in case he had to stop and speak. He held his head high, disguising his real feelings, inwardly cursing the arrival of the train and the incompetence of the starter who caused him to make the false start. The noisy train and the long wait for the gun had ruined his concentration.

Cec had been penalised by being put back two yards for the restart. The starter was following Amateur Athletic Association (AAA) rules, even though this junior race at a town fair would never have been registered with them. Fearing further penalty or even disqualification if he repeated the offence, Cec had been slow off the line.

He had needed to get away quickly. The handicap distance given to the other runners meant he had a lot of catching up to do, and in his effort to reach the front had tried to do too much too early. The grass track was short with tight bends that would have slowed his rivals, so Cec should have been more patient and trusted his raw pace. Instead, he charged through the field and was tripped by a rival who went on to win. Cec immediately picked himself up and aggressively tore through the pack a second time, but he was left with too much ground to make up in such a short race.

Cec caught the leader on the line but failed to pass him. He collapsed exhausted. He had run his hardest and the crowd recognised it, cheering in appreciation at the dramatic finish that had unfolded before their eyes.

The stewards considered the clash between them to be a racing incident, but Cec knew otherwise. Once recovered he remonstrated against the winner but he had his friends nearby, so all Cec received for his effort was abuse. They knew he was not likely to retaliate with his fists – Cec was known for his quiet nature and slight build – so they taunted him, making hurtful comments about the absence of his family, which made the bitterness of his loss even worse.

Realising that his argument was in vain, Cec retreated home. The route from the playing field to his house in London Road took him by The Gnoll, the ground of Neath Rugby Football Club. It was hallowed turf as far his family were concerned. His spirits lifted as he approached the empty ground and he imagined the roar of the crowd mixed with harmonious singing. Many times he had gone to matches with his father and immersed himself in the exciting atmosphere. After every game they took the same route home along Gnoll Park Road. As he retraced their footsteps, he recalled a conversation they often had.

'Hey Cec, did I tell you about how the All Blacks copied our strip?'*

'Yes father,' Cec would reply with a smile, knowing he was going to hear it again anyway.

'When New Zealand formed their national team they were discussing what colour strip they should wear. Somebody asked, "Which is the greatest rugby team in the world?" Well, Neath was the only answer, wasn't it? So the New Zealanders decided to adopt our all-black strip.' With obvious affection, his father added, 'That was a great mark of respect for our team, wasn't it son?'

The imagined presence of Cec's father was so powerful that tears streamed down his cheeks. Cec missed him so much and was still sobbing when he reached London Road.

Relieved to be home, Cec sat down at the kitchen table without saying a word to his mother, who was preparing

---

* There are various theories about the naming of the New Zealand team. One alternative explanation is that during their British tour in 1905 their forwards had played like backs and a misprinted headline in the press referred to them as All Blacks instead of All Backs. Another version is that they once played in a black strip as a mark of respect following the death of a player. However, their strip was predominately black before the time of both of these incidents, so perhaps Cec's father was correct.

the scraps of meat she had brought home from work. She noticed with concern his flushed cheeks.

'What's wrong Cec? Is everything alright?'

He was self-conscious and embarrassed by her question. 'Of course mother, I ran home.'

Cec may have failed to win his uncle's silver shillings, but he put the certificate for second place down on the table. She picked it up and carefully examined it.

'You've done well. Tell me all about it.' She sat down opposite him, anticipating his account. As always, it would be meticulous in every detail.

*

Cec grew up not knowing much about his father – it is even possible his mother was unaware of her husband's early life. Benjamin Griffiths was born in August 1860 in Westminster, where he lived with his parents and three elder sisters; Mary, Maria and Martha, in the parish of St James. His father, also named Benjamin, and his mother, Elizabeth, were both from Neath. Benjamin Senior's work as a tailor likely took them to the capital, so far away from home. In 1865, Elizabeth died and the family was torn apart, never to be reunited. The three young girls were sent back to Neath to work as domestic servants while father and son moved into St James' Workhouse on Poland Street, not far from their old home.

Life would have been very tough for Benjamin, existing alongside 150 other residents in the institution, many of them foreign refugees. For the bereft young boy, still only five years old, it was a cruel punishment after losing his mother. Escape from the workhouse only came ten years later, joining the Royal Navy in 1875 when he was just fifteen, lying about his age so he was accepted as a sixteen-year-old boy seaman. His service record showed his birth date as 15 June 1859, a discrepancy of more than a year.

Benjamin excelled in his new-found freedom and within three years had reached able seaman status, with excellent and very good levels of performance on his service record at every stage of his life at sea, predominately on HMS *Agincourt*. One of only two photographs of him that survives shows him still just a boy in his naval uniform. His *Agincourt* cap band and the chevrons he wore on his arm, denoting good conduct, were his most treasured possessions. After Benjamin died, Cec kept them in a tiny cloth bag which became hidden in a cleft of the briefcase containing his own collection of cloth badges and running shirts.*

HMS *Agincourt* was a 10,000 ton ironclad battleship of the Minotaur Class with five masts as well as a steam engine and propellers. She was an elegant ship, magnificent under full sail and reflected the fully-rigged ocean tea clippers that had dominated the world's trading routes for several decades. However, even as Benjamin climbed aboard for the first time, the accelerating nature of the Industrial Revolution meant that hybrid vessels like the *Agincourt* would soon be obsolete.

Steam power had developed over the past decades and sail power was becoming outdated. *Cutty Sark* may still have been breaking speed records, but seeking out the winds was fraught with the dangers of gales and storms. On the other

---

* I discovered them in the latter stages of preparing this book. Only because of my research into Benjamin's life was their significance immediately realised.

hand, becoming stranded in the Doldrums, the area around the equator between the two belts of trade winds, could herald a financial disaster for ship owners. The dawning of the new industrial age unshackled the Royal Navy from the vagaries of the weather, where a favourable wind was necessary to gain a strategic advantage. Steam power and better guns made the business of warfare at sea more remote as ships could engage in battle from a distance.

Benjamin excelled with the cutlass and was committed to the seafaring way of life when he signed up for a ten year Continuous Service Arrangement in 1877, so it must have been a hard blow when he was invalided out of the Royal Navy with epilepsy in 1880. Nevertheless, by the time Benjamin left, his skills with the cutlass were no longer necessary and his ship's fighting days were over. They both drifted towards new horizons to play out the rest of their lives peaceably.

Benjamin returned to civilian life with just a kit bag and the clothes he stood up in. He probably came to Neath to join his relocated sisters and worked hard to establish himself there, ultimately finding work as an insurance agent. In June 1888, he was elected on to the busy committee of Neath RFC. The minutes of the meetings regularly held at the Crown Hotel show he was considerably involved with the day-to-day running of the club, ranging from financial aspects to the behaviour of the players. Benjamin was even called upon to referee matches as far away as Hull.

At the committee meeting on 19 November 1888, Benjamin seconded a motion to discipline George Trick following his poor conduct towards the referee at Penarth. This motion could have had a bad effect on Benjamin's love life – his future wife, Sarah, was the player's sister.* Surely it was the rugby club which caused their paths to cross, although whether their relationship started before or after this disciplinary matter is unknown.

Sarah Trick's family were originally farmers from Holsworthy in north Devon. Her father, William, had uprooted his wife, four daughters (including Sarah) and three sons in 1870 from their farm to Briton Ferry Road, Neath, where they had another son and daughter. It was a case of the grass being greener (and only just visible) on the other side of the Bristol Channel. William bought a butcher's shop, the sons worked on local farms and ten-year-old Sarah went to work as a live-in servant with the Quick family of Lincoln Place.

By 1881, William Trick had bought his own farm and 21-year-old Sarah was working there as a dairy maid, living with her parents. Despite their move from their Devon cattle farm, the Trick family was still toiling in the same business. Perhaps the grass on the northern side of the Bristol Channel wasn't that much greener, after all.

Aside from the common bond of rugby, Sarah and Benjamin would have had empathy with the other's hard upbringing. The ingredients for them to get on were there in abundance and chemistry provided the passion, so it was inevitable love would soon follow, not always the case in a Victorian marriage.

---

* The Trick family produced several successful sportsmen and women, so it is likely Cec inherited his sporting prowess from his mother's side. Aside from George, who would go on to become a popular captain of the first team, the family included Stan Trick, grandson of Sarah's sister, who played cricket for Glamorgan between 1946 and 1950 and football for Wales as a schoolboy.

Benjamin was promoted to insurance superintendent and was able to buy a house at 79 London Road when he married Sarah in 1892. Benjamin named it Agincourt House in memory of his beloved ship. For a few precious years he would find fulfilment at the solid, terraced Victorian house in Neath, his first proper home since he was five.

Benjamin and his bride were both 32 when they married – not that Benjamin knew that. He thought Sarah was two years younger. In uptight Victorian society, marrying a younger man could be frowned upon. Sarah invented a birth date to make her appear 30 years old and kept this secret for the rest of her life. The proof is in her own hand on the 1911 census, when as head of the household she entered her age incorrectly.

Benjamin lived for only sixteen years after marrying Sarah. Their brief time together was largely happy, although tragedy was a common visitor to the household. Of their six children, three died as infants, one living for only three minutes.[*]

The first of the three survivors, Ben Burrows Paige Griffiths, was born in 1893. In keeping with family tradition he was christened with an abridged version of his father's name. Eva Daisy Charlotte Griffiths was their third child

[*] If it hadn't been for the eventual discovery of a family Bible and its inscriptions, finding information about the dead children would have been near impossible due to the overwhelming volume of records to be researched. During the first decade of the twentieth century there were 450 children born with the surname Griffiths in Neath. 80 (18%) died before reaching the age of one. This was double the national average and reflected the impoverished industrial nature of South Wales, where most men worked down the mines or in the steel industry. Advances in medical care improved public health after the First World War; a similar survey of the 270 Griffiths children born in Neath in the 1930s shows the death rate reduced considerably, with only 17 perishing prior to their first birthday - less than 7%.

in 1897; Cec was the fifth, three years later. They were all educated at the local Gnoll School where Cec won his first race, a junior 100 yards sprint open to all schoolchildren in the town to mark the coronation of King George V on 22 June 1911. Little did Cec's family know where that first win would eventually lead him.

The Griffiths family maintained a good standard of living and even employed a young girl called Margaret Francis as a live-in servant, but cruel fate suddenly turned their lives upside down in 1906. Benjamin contracted tuberculosis, a potentially lethal disease in the early twentieth century, and suffered badly for the last two years of his life. Medical advice suggested that he live in a warm, dry climate and Benjamin planned to move his family to South Africa, but he rapidly deteriorated and died in March 1908 before the move could be achieved. Sarah was left in turmoil – would the move have saved him, or would he still have died, leaving the family stranded in a foreign country?

Just like his own father, Cec had lost a parent at a young age. Benjamin was able to rebuild his life and succeed through hard work in the face of adversity. Cec would need to do the same.

Cec and Eva were christened on 17 May 1906 at St David's Church in Neath. They were unusually old to be christened, but in the face of their father's life-threatening diagnosis it might have been the stark realisation of Benjamin's mortality which made the family look towards God for a solution. It is not known if the family had a strong faith to sustain them through the crisis following his death, but Cec attended Sunday school at St Thomas' Church and in 1907 won a prize of a prayer book for 'regular attendance, punctuality and good conduct'. It would be these fine qualities and his strength of character which would see him through difficult times ahead. He was confirmed at St David's Church on 4 December 1914 and presented with another prayer book in which he wrote 'Always at my Duty, Daily on my knees, Often round the Altar'.

He wrote the same words in the family Bible, followed by the following passage from Archbishop Thomas Cranmer's 1549 Book of Common Prayer:

> ALMYGHTYE God, give us grace, that we may cast awaye the workes of darknes and put upon us the armour of light, now in the tyme of this mortall lyfe, (in the whiche thy sonne Jesus Christe came to visite us in great humilitie;) that in the last daye when he shal come again in this glorious majestye to judge bothe the quicke and the dead, we maye ryse to the lyfe immortal, through him who liveth and reigneth with thee and the holy ghoste now and ever. Amen.

But religion and prayer would not put food on the table. After Benjamin's death, Sarah worked at the family butcher shop, then run by her brother George. The luxury of a live-in servant had to go, and the spare bed was taken by a boarder, Herbert Miles, whose rent was a valuable addition to the family coffers. Ben had attended Neath Grammar School before his father died, but that was no longer possible for Cec. He needed to get a job and earn some money for the household. That need became even more urgent when war broke out in 1914. The black market was thriving, prices had gone up for everything and nobody was going to help them but themselves.

When Cec left school at the age of fourteen, he was lucky to walk straight into a job in the Divisional Superintendent's office at the Great Western Railway depot in Neath. Two massive sheds accommodated turntables and serviced 120 locomotives run by the company. Employment was scarce in the shrinking economy and Cec had his Uncle William, who would later put up the prizes for the race he would run in 1915, to thank for his good fortune. As a former Mayor of Neath, town councillor and prominent local businessman, William had considerable influence in the area so finding a position for his nephew had not been difficult. It would not be the only time William would help Cec at a pivotal juncture in his life.

*

There was a knock at the door. Cec, still smarting over his defeat in the Great September Fair race, grudgingly got up to answer it while his mother prepared the meal. It was an old friend, Ivor Rees, wearing the uniform of the Royal Welch Fusiliers, who Cec had not seen since the war started. Ivor was more than two years his senior and looked even older in uniform. He was also somewhat heavier, probably due to the army grub. With him was a petite girl with auburn hair and fair skin like porcelain. Cec recognised her as Ivor's sister, Gladys, but everybody knew her by her middle name, May.

She spoke first. 'Do you remember me? I met you at The Gnoll before the war when we went to watch Neath play.'

It all came back to him. On the day in question, Ivor had brought some of his family to a match, including his sister.

Cec recalled her as being pretty but quiet and one year his junior. Now she stood facing him, Cec realised she had grown up considerably since then.

'Yes, of course I remember.' The words came out abruptly and he felt a little embarrassed. The change in her held him transfixed, stumbling over his words.

Ivor stepped in to save him. 'I joined up when I was eighteen. I've finished my training and have two days leave before being sent to the Western Front.'

Cec tried to think of the right thing to say. This time his mother saved him, shouting from the kitchen, 'Aren't you going to ask them in?'

They all sat down while Sarah made tea. Ivor again led the conversation. 'May came to meet me at the station and told me about your great run.'

'It wasn't that great. I lost,' Cec said, curtly.

May was indignant in disagreeing. 'At the start of the race I was the only one cheering you. At the end everybody was.'

'May said it was the most magnificent thing she had ever seen,' Ivor added.

As May picked up the certificate, Cec noticed her tiny, delicate fingers and exquisite narrow wrists. She threw it back down, dismissively. 'This doesn't mean a thing. I saw everything you did today. You should feel proud. It took some nerve to confront him afterwards.'

Cec went light-headed and thought he was going to faint. His emotions were in turmoil. He was embarrassed by the praise being heaped on him, he was annoyed at his own reticence and inability to say the right thing, but he knew he didn't want this feisty and attractive girl to leave.

Cec's mother was watching and listening with interest. She asked Ivor and May to stay for supper, but they politely refused because Ivor had such little time to see his own family as it was.

As they were about to leave, Ben and Eva arrived home with some food for the meal. Ben had not volunteered for military service because of the family's precarious financial situation and his mother was concerned that he might be embarrassed by seeing Ivor in their house. A 21-year-old man was expected to be seen in public wearing military uniform, not the well-groomed attire that Ben picked up from the clothes shop he worked in, and the attention that Ben's dress sense garnered was not always the right kind. Men who did not volunteer were deemed as shirkers and suffered demeaning abuse, receiving white feathers symbolising cowardice in the post or being handed them by women in the street.

Young men, the pride of Wales, were sent to the battlefields in huge numbers, many to be sacrificed in futile attacks. One of May and Ivor's other brothers, Trevor, had been in the vanguard of the fighting with the South Wales Borderers since the start of the war. Another of her brothers, Emlyn, would soon be following in Trevor and Ivor's footsteps. As May and Ivor talked about their three brothers fighting shoulder to shoulder for their country, the emotion of the moment became too much for May to cope with. What Cec did next was driven by natural instinct – if he had thought too much about it, he would never have had the courage to do it.

He had never held a girl before, but as she sobbed he gently embraced her and she cried on his shoulder, holding him tightly. At last, Cec had managed to get over his tongue-tied nervousness to offer reassuring words. 'Come on, don't worry, Ivor will be fine,' he said, trying to sound convincing. 'Remember how he looked after himself on the rugby pitch. We fought some pretty big battles there.'

Now on a roll, Cec tried to make use of the moment.

'I am running at Pontypridd in a few weeks. Would you like to come with me?' he blurted out as they let go of each other. His stomach leapt with the realisation she might refuse his invitation in front of his entire family.

She looked at him for a second before replying. 'Yes, I would like to.'

They met up whenever possible over the next few months, but it was not easy for May to get away from her household chores. She had six brothers and two much older sisters. Her youngest brother, Idris, had never been well since his birth in 1908 during which their mother died. It was left to the three girls to take on the role of looking after the house and their little brother. Her father and several brothers who lived at home were engine fitters and blacksmiths, exempt from war service, so the household duties were demanding. Washing the men's heavily soiled clothes, scouring the shops for enough food to cook and cleaning from dawn to dusk left her with little time for herself.

May's apparent fragility belied a deep resilience and toughness which had brought her through a motherless childhood in a predominately male environment with sisters too old to play with her. She looked forward to her occasional trip out with Cec, even though it often involved standing by the side of a running track getting cold and wet in the Welsh summer.

Cec in the uniform of the Queen's Westminster Rifles

3

CECIL'S
WAR
1916-1918

Cec had a promising career in rugby snuffed out by the combination of leaving school early and the war, which forced a curtailment of sport. While at school his natural sporting talent, speed and eye for the ball ensured a place in the Neath RFC junior team, and a position in the senior team, following in his Uncle George's footsteps, would surely have been certain. His early life coincided with the golden age of Welsh rugby which kicked off in 1905 when the national team narrowly and controversially beat the seemingly undefeatable touring All Blacks at Cardiff Arms Park. He remembered his father at his most joyous after the game, a result which was celebrated in their household alongside just about every home in Wales. The end of this glorious chapter of Welsh sport came with an ignominious match in the Five Nations Championship in March 1914, against Ireland in Belfast. It was brutal at best, descending into running fist fights on the pitch. The Welsh forwards were dubbed the Terrible Eight by the press and the match entered the annals of rugby as one of the most violent internationals ever held. It was a chilling prelude to the hostility soon to be unleashed on murderous battlefields throughout the world.

With rugby no longer a serious option, Cec kept fit by walking and running in his local area. He had the freedom of the Vale of Neath, with its waterfalls and wooded hills offering him some of the most scenic countryside in Wales to explore. One of his favourite strolls – or more likely runs – was the round trip of five miles along the Neath and Tennant Canals between his home and Aberdulais. The circular route took him less than an hour and he did it nearly every day to keep fit and counteract the lethargy of sitting for hours in the office at the Great Western Railway depot.

However, Cec does not appear to have seriously followed up the race in which he finished second at the Great September Fair. His new romance and work commitments precluded him pursuing running more earnestly. Local races were usually held on a Saturday when he worked at the railway depot, and he saw May on Sundays after they went to church, so there wasn't much time left for competitive running.

Cec occupied what remained of his spare time drawing and writing; one lengthy rhyme in his neat handwriting on faded letter paper appears to be of his own creation. If so, it demonstrates a degree of devilment and wit:

My Mother says I'm naughty, but I really can't see why,
She says I must be better, and I always say I'll try.
Then she says, "Remember you must try with all your might."
But out of all the things I do, so few of them seem right.
I had a smacking yesterday for smashing a few eggs
and another later for sticking pins in Grandpa's legs.
I didn't mean to do it and I'm sorry if it hurt,
I really only meant to pin his trousers to his shirt.
And then I got in trouble 'cos I spoilt my Granny's bonnet,
She laid it on the sofa and I went and sat upon it.
But it wasn't my fault was it, it shouldn't have been there.
When I get blamed for things like this, I hardly think it's fair.
Then Dad got in a rage with me for denting his new hat,
I was only playing lessons and a Parson's hat is flat.
It really does seem hard on me, I never get a rest,
my oldest sister's young man says that I'm a proper pest.
Some chewing gum of mine got lost as I thought in the street,
but then I saw it sticking to my sister's young man's seat.
When I told him how it was there and asked him for it back,
he got in such a temper that he gave me quite a whack.
The man next door, he scowls at me as if I were some tramp,
The lady there is worse, she says that I'm a little scamp.
And all because I threw a stone at what I thought was a mouse
And missed it, the stone went through a pane in their glasshouse.
Mum and the lady the other side are not on friendly terms,
when I think how I'm blamed for that my little body squirms.

Just after they went there to live, one day I said to her,
"Please tell me Mrs Simpkins, can you me-ow and purr?"
She looked at me and then she said, "What makes you ask
me that?"
I said, "I heard Mum telling Dad that you're a proper cat."
If anything goes wrong it's little me who gets the blame,
and if I didn't do it I get a whacking just the same.
Dad says he cannot understand how one can cause such trouble
And cuffed me when I said, "Well Dad, perhaps I've got a
double."

Cec and Ben both enjoyed drawing and their humorous style, often using the military as the butt of their jokes, was very similar. There is only one example of Cec's cartoons that survives, dated June 1917, but examples of Ben's are more numerous and contained in two albums. Also on those pages are sketches and prose created by soldiers recovering at Gnoll Park Hospital in Neath during 1917 and 1918. The albums were probably taken into the hospital by Herbert Miles, the Griffiths' lodger, a dental mechanic whose skills would have been essential in the rebuilding of men's shattered faces. Some of the drawings are exquisite; the words are witty, moving and often critical of controversial events at the time. The execution of the British nurse, Edith Cavell, by the Germans in 1915 was still a bitter memory. The ability of the soldiers to express their feelings in drawings and the written word must have provided some psychological relief. Whether Ben and Herbert realised the extent of the emotional support they offered is unknown.*

* Several of the entries provide significant information about the men who made them and it is my intention to try and trace their families utilising regimental records to show them these very personal cameos.

Even though first-class sport had been put on hold with so many men away fighting, there were frequent fundraising events for the war effort involving any combination of boxing, five-a-side football, cycling, horse trials, whippet racing, shooting, tug of war and athletics. These mixed sporting events would be heavily advertised for weeks ahead in the *South Wales Daily Post* and the *South Wales Echo* with promises of grand prizes to be awarded to attract as many entrants as possible. Competitors had to pay an entrance fee, typically a shilling, as would friends and families coming to watch. They would have parted with more money on refreshments and side shows in further support of the good cause. Money and sport were rare commodities at the time, so to raise one by using the other was a popular activity for all concerned.

Most of these events were held to raise funds for the Volunteer Training Corps, an unarmed militia made up of those passed over for regular military service by age or fitness. The VTC was responsible for defending towns if the Germans invaded; a similar role to the Home Guard of the Second World War. Quite how they were expected to achieve their objective before they were armed with rifles in 1917 is unclear. Indeed, the Army seems to have viewed the VTC with some derision – their uniforms were deliberately different and all equipment had to be funded privately. However, one undoubted benefit of the VTC was its boost to morale; the involvement of civilians in their own defence would have given them a sense of purpose and worth.

Some of these events offered competitors a chance of going home with bulging pockets. An event at Ammanford Recreation Ground some twenty miles from Neath, on 2

October 1915, offered £7 to the winner of the 150 yards handicap race. In 1915 it would have taken an agricultural labourer more than a month to earn such a sum. This was an enterprise intended to attract professional runners and would have been avoided by amateurs who understood and feared the possible consequences if they took part.

One of the races with a more reasonable prize pot was held in the grounds of Neath Abbey on 28 July 1917. The Skewen and Neath Abbey Grand Sports was intended to raise funds for B Company of the 4th Battalion of the Glamorgan Voluntary Reserve, the VTC unit commanded by Cec's uncle, Major William Trick. Perhaps William persuaded Cec to take part for a bit of fun simply because he was family, without any comprehension that he might win. Cec was still young and unknown outside of his immediate circle of friends and family. The Great September Fair race two years previous where he met May remained the biggest event that he had competed in.

It was a typical carnival with emphasis on enjoyment rather than winning. The organisers had provided a varied range of activities with cash prizes on offer. The battalion band and the Glyn Neath Silver Band provided entertainment. There was an obstacle race, tug of war, tilting the bucket, point to point, several events for wounded soldiers and two running races open to all which attracted some serious competitors. It was in one of these that, probably for the first time ever, Cec's name appeared in print for breaking the worsted cord.

Cec was running off a 38 yards head start in a 440 yards open handicap race, which meant the distance he actually covered was 402 yards. Considering his ability, this was a generous allowance, reflecting the fact that Cec had a lack of known form and was a newcomer to open-age races. However, Cec was not the only one given an advantage – William Edwards from Ystalyfera was running off 53 yards, so Cec had at least one other competitor to overtake on his way to victory.

Success at Neath Abbey was the catalyst which prompted his arrival on the Welsh athletics scene. The £3 prize was the biggest lump sum Cec had ever earned, and he was spurred to try and replicate it at other events. Was Cec's win down to the luck of an unknown athlete being given a generous handicap? Not likely. Just over a month later, Wales' grandest carnival of the war was held over three days at Victoria Park in Swansea, providing the usual athletics and football challenges with cash prizes to attract big entries. To maintain an interest for all age groups, there were races for boys under fourteen, novelty events including pillow fighting and sack racing, exciting demonstrations in high diving and also a display in timbering. The event was held in aid of Swansea Hospital which owed over £8,000 to its creditors. They sent out an urgent message to the inhabitants of the city: 'lend us your aid.' The appeal did not fall on deaf ears. An excited crowd of 25,000 packed into the park to enjoy the entertainment and well over £3,000 was raised to help reduce their debts.

500 competitors took part in the athletics alone, including sixty runners in the 100 yards and forty in the 440 yards races, all of whom paid a shilling entrance fee. Cec came through the heats in both. He finished third in the 100 yards and earned a £1 prize. In the 440 yards, he finished first for

the second time in a matter of weeks. He took home £3 prize money again, this time coupled with a large silver cup. For an unknown local lad to carry off such large winner's spoils from under the hard noses of professional runners was an outstanding and unexpected achievement.

As the end of the year approached, Cec's run of success was still not over. On 20 October in a mixed athletics and cycling event in aid of the local Soldiers' Reception Fund at The Gnoll, he won another 440 yards open handicap with a reduced advantage of 27 yards. On this occasion – as was usually the case – the prizes awarded were not divulged in the press reports and Cec's winnings are unknown.

In those races of 1917, Cec ran as he only knew how. He was quick off the line and maintained an even but rapid pace throughout. It worked out well for him, but he had no tactical strategy to make the most of his ability or experience to counter the strengths and weaknesses of his rivals.

Cec's success was beginning to draw attention to him – but not all the comments he received were welcome. After one particular prize giving, a smartly-dressed man about 50 years old with the manner and looks of an Army officer or a government official approached Cec. In a quiet voice he said, 'You shouldn't have taken that prize lad. Best if you had stayed at home and let the others fight it out.'

His tone was business-like. Perhaps there was even a hint of threat about it. But before Cec could respond, the man turned and briskly walked away with an easy stride to disappear amongst the crowd.

Cec was unsettled by the encounter, wondering who the mysterious man was. The more he contemplated the stranger's words, the more he was puzzled by them. Initially, Cec thought the man was just a disgruntled spectator, perhaps supporting one of the beaten runners. Yet his lack of emotion and his English accent made that unlikely, and nobody knew who he was. Further enquiries revealed that he had been spotted throughout the afternoon taking notes after each race and at the prize giving. He did not seem to have spoken a word to anyone except Cec. Why had he been singled out? The incident troubled him for some time, but the continuing war would make such worries pale into insignificance.

*

As the war progressed (or more accurately staggered from one bloody stalemate to the next) the need for new men to replenish the devastated ranks became more and more urgent. In January 1916, the Military Service Act introduced conscription of single men aged 18 to 41 to the armed forces.

Cec's brother, Ben, was eligible for service during the war, yet he appears to have spent it safely in Neath. Unlike many of May's brothers, he wasn't in a reserved occupation. No infirmity was declared, and since he lived a healthy life until he died aged 69 of a heart attack and was a successful businessman, accomplished tennis player and bowls champion, it is unlikely he received a medical exemption.

It is possible he avoided conscription on grounds of him being the main provider in the Griffiths family, responsible for the care of his widowed mother and two younger siblings. Possibly he joined lodger Herbert Miles in working at the Gnoll Park Hospital in Neath – that would certainly explain why soldiers used his albums for their drawings and writings.

Military tribunals were held to decide on such applications on compassionate grounds. The workload of the tribunal officials in dealing with the applications, many contrived, was considerable. Whatever the claims that Ben had to avoid service, he had one great thing in his favour. His respected uncle, Major William Trick, was on the panel of the Neath and Glamorgan tribunals. Cec may not have been the only one to have benefited from their uncle's position and influence in the town.

There is a variation to this theory which portrays William Burrows Trick's nepotism less favourably. Neath had high regard for its councillor, Justice of the Peace and ex-mayor. Yet Clement Robert Trueman, who had a shop beside William Trick's Auctioneers and Valuers, was a voice championing loudly the fight against wrongdoing by council officials. He certainly didn't like his neighbour, who he called 'Trickie Billie, King of Neath'. Clement was of the opinion that William and another ex-mayor, Hopkin Morgan, were repeatedly guilty of swindling, lying and hypocrisy.

Clement was a photographer and his skills as a poet and artist provided him with the means to produce a series of postcards which were crammed with innuendo and accusations of theft, fraud or abuse of position. He was a regular visitor to the law courts facing libel charges, but that never deterred him and he continued with his public spirited campaigns. 'W.B.T.' was his prime target.

His accusations against William were quite specific. Clement claimed that William was sheltering his own relatives from conscription by providing employment for them on the family's farm at Penlan as potato pickers, protecting them like a mother goose. As Chairman of the Neath Tribunal, he would then preside over their applications for military exemption on the grounds that as agricultural workers their occupations were reserved. This could have been precisely the reason why Ben did not serve in the armed services. William's alleged conduct in the treatment of his own sons – and possibly his nephew Ben, who shared his uncle's middle name – was at odds with his military background and VTC responsibilities. This was guaranteed to provoke another of Clement's crusades. The product of his grievance was the *The Penlan Geese*, a postcard which was abundantly detailed, symbolic and unreservedly critical of William's allegedly corrupt role in protecting his family.[*]

As Cec approached his eighteenth birthday in February 1918 with war still raging, he understood what fate had in store for him. Cec was a natural pacifist. He had never hurt anybody and was haunted by the knowledge that so many of his young generation were already just a memory in the minds of their loved ones.

The battles of Ypres, Somme, Verdun, Arras, Passchendaele and many more had left a bloody butcher's bill. At this

[*] The existence of Clement Trueman's postcard was discovered at Neath Library where I met Harriet Eaton, Heritage Education Officer, who was a great help researching Cec and his family. She was already familiar with William Trick as such a pivotal character in Neath's history – it transpired she was passionately interested in Clement Trueman and his 33 controversial postcards. Harriet had managed to trace Clement's great-grandson, Clive Trueman, and in a remarkable coincidence their first meeting occurred on my trip to the library. *The Penlan Geese* postcard raised as many questions as it answered, but Clive brought the history to life by explaining much of its meaning and symbolism. He gave credence to the theory that Ben may have indeed benefitted from William's position.

late stage in the war, a collective idea was coalescing that fine young men were being thrown headlong into a maelstrom by autocratic politicians and generals who only measured success or failure by the amount of muddy ground taken, regardless of the length of the casualty list. It didn't take long for the dreadful carnage of battle to make the patriotic recruits recognise reality.

The Great September Fair in 1915 would always hold a special place in the hearts of Cec and May because it was the occasion that led to their meeting. But for one soldier, it was a far more fateful event. On the Sunday morning after the fair, a goods train driver found the body of Private Robert Stephens, a single man from Llwynypia serving with the 25th Battalion of the Welsh Regiment, on the railway line at Pembrey in Carmarthenshire. There were several accounts of young infantry men from Glamorgan who took their lives in a similar fashion. Others shot themselves. Cec would have been aware of these local tragedies and was alert to the reasons which made a traumatised soldier on leave, cocooned by the safety and familiarity of his family, take the only course of action he considered would end his torment and suffering. Cec was a realist with a keen understanding of what was really happening in France and Belgium. It was obvious he would soon be called up to serve his country.

Life – his life – was precious. He was not prepared to throw it away. He had a job at the railway. He had a girl-friend whom he had been courting for over two years. As boyhood gave way to manhood, it was sad but not surprising that he slipped into a trough of worried despair which lasted for several months and robbed him of his youthful vitality.

May was worried about Cec and wondered whether their relationship would survive the strain.

Again, Uncle William seemed to offer Cec a way out. William, who had been a major in the Territorial Army, still had influence within military circles. He managed to secure his nephew's entry to the Queen's Westminster Rifles, a Territorial regiment in London, to pre-empt anything worse. The QWR also had a fine sporting tradition, especially athletics. Perhaps there was an ulterior motive for Cec's involvement in athletics competitions shortly before his imminent call up, boosting his chances of being accepted by his preferred regiment.

Whatever the case, Cec was accepted and would soon be making his first foray across the border into England. As was quite usual for the time, especially when the country was at war, Cec did not travel far from his home as he grew up. Trips to Swansea were probably as far afield as he went. The chance to mix with men from all over the country and to see the capital city must have been awe-inspiring.

Cec moved to London after his eighteenth birthday in February 1918 for training as a rifleman. Fortunately for him, an extension to the Military Service Act in April 1918 dictated that soldiers had to be aged at least 18 years and 6 months to be sent overseas and had to have six months of training. This provided a valuable cushion of extra time before Cec would face the German guns. His mother must have prayed for the war to be over before his time was up.

The need for British soldiers had never been higher than in 1918. In the spring, the German Army, fearing that American troops pouring into the Western Front would make their position hopeless, launched Operation Michael, a major offensive using elite stormtroopers to attack the British lines held by the Fifth Army. Allied losses were so heavy that the front line was pushed back forty miles in the Somme area. British military commanders had been made sluggish by three years of static warfare and were unprepared for such dynamic tactics, losing control as the enemy rapidly gained ground.

Men undergoing training had little doubt where their destiny lay. Basic training was intended to build up physical fitness, instil discipline, instruct in the use of weapons and teach marching drills. Sport was encouraged by the Army to foster team building. Cec already had a head start on many in the sporting sphere and quickly threw himself into athletics at the battalion and brigade sports events.

He had been recruited to the 3/16th County of London Battalion (QWR) billeted on Wimbledon Common. This reserve battalion was responsible for supplying trained men to the two active battalions of the Queen's Westminster Rifles to replace battle casualties, so the posting was only a temporary one. The recruits were able to enjoy the proximity of the capital, but the clock was always ticking until they would be summoned to the front.

For Cec, it was time to take his destiny into his own hands and decide his future. He needed to prove his value to his regiment as an athlete.

As Cec was about to embark on his athletics career, an influential character in his life was still relatively early in his career as an athletics writer. Joe Binks was the *News of the World* athletics correspondent, a post he held for 54 years (he died in 1966 aged 92). He was certainly a respected voice in the sport – during his own successful running career he had broken the British record for the mile, taking it with 4:16.8 in 1902, a time which was still yet to be beaten in 1918.

During wartime, Binks formed strong links with the military and organised their inter-services athletics meetings in London. The next meeting was the Southfields Military Charity Sports Carnival at Croydon in July 1918 – exactly when Cec's posting overseas was due and the demand for men at the front was most pressing.

Cec, encouraged by his army pals who recognised his running ability, paid a visit one evening to Joe at his home in Wandsworth. In his newspaper column, Joe described the meeting:

> C.R. Griffiths... came to see me and asked if he and his mates could run at a military sports meeting I was organising at Southfields. Griffiths who looked a frail sort of youth – he was only 17 [sic] – requested me not to give him a big start, for he could run a bit, and wished his mates, who were not runners, to have a chance. This was my first meeting with Griffiths, and for his honesty, handicapper W.J. Pepper and myself awarded him 35 yards start in the open 880 yards.

The field was a strong one, made up of some very capable athletes from a wide range of military units. Joe was not confident about Cec's ability to win, admitting, 'We certainly thought he had something to do, but he ran through the field in amazing style winning very easily.'

Joe became Cec's first friend and adviser in the athletics world. Many times in his column he took the credit for discovering him. He never forgot the unselfish generous nature of Cec which 'summed up the fine type of amateur he was all through his career' – ironic words in view of what would happen to him later.

Joe was so impressed with Cec that he immediately entered him in the Stamford Bridge Holiday Carnival, an event to select the English (in effect British) team to compete against a host of countries in the forthcoming Inter-Services Championship. Cec justified his inclusion, scoring a 'brilliant win' in the 880 yards and putting forward a convincing case for his selection in the England team.

In the 440 yards Cec found himself up against the burly and experienced New Zealand champion, Corporal J.L. 'Dan' Mason. It was the first time Cec had lined up alongside world-class opposition. Mason had been a successful professional runner in his home country before serving with distinction as a volunteer in the trenches of the Western Front. He became a member of the New Zealand Army running team and competed in over forty events during 1918 and 1919 in Europe where he was only beaten twice. At the time he lined up against Cec, he was unbeaten.

Cec made 28-year-old Mason work hard for his narrow win on a loose track in a time of 51 seconds. His young Welsh challenger must have given him quite a fright, battling along the home straight side by side, champion runner and young unknown.

Just a few days later, at the same venue, they met again in the Inter-Services Championship. The world's best military athletes battled it out in an international championship and there was an innovative idea of allowing the public to attend without paying. This ensured a large turnout to witness the likes of the Blue Streak, Australian sprinter Sergeant Jack Donaldson – although he failed to deliver the expected win. Home-grown heroes such as Hon. H.R. Alexander and Fred Mawby were among the entrants who received a fine tribute from the press:

> Competitors, almost without exception, carried scars from the battlefields, and only an inborn love of healthy exercise, which in many cases had carried them through the fights, and the desire to keep fit, permitted such a state of affairs.

Athletic News described Cec as one of the few unknowns on view, and his 440 yards races with some of the well-known men were classics. In the heat his 'really clever judgement' enabled him to 'run the legs' off Captain Hodges and Lieutenant Davidson halfway down the home stretch for victory. In the final, his task was more difficult. Fred Mawby, Hampshire's champion and war hero, led for the first 80 yards. Then the formidable Mason forged to the front. He led until 'Griffiths, within 25 yards of the tape, slipped past the bunch on the outside and tackled the big Colonial after the manner of a seasoned veteran'. In doing so, he became the first man to beat Mason during the war. The picture of Cec breaking the tape inches ahead of Mason is the earliest one of him racing. *Athletic News* reported his performance was the best of the afternoon and boldly stated, 'He must be regarded as an embryo champion, unless good judges are much mistaken.'

Cec's winning time of 51.2 seconds was 0.2 seconds slower than Mason's victory a few days earlier. Mason must have been suffering from weary legs having won the mile just an hour earlier; later in the day he would also triumph in the half mile. Nevertheless, for Cec it was a sweet victory. He had comfortably stepped up from local Welsh races to show that he was at home on the international stage.

When Cec came home on leave in September 1918 to attend his brother's wedding, the *South Wales Echo* featured him with a photograph in uniform, describing his successes running for the Army in London. They were very proud of their local hero who had beaten some famous athletes, returning home laden with the trophies he had won.[*]

Ben's wedding on 24 September 1918 to Lilian Thomas, five years his senior, at the Neath Parish Church of St David's was witnessed by Cecil and Eva. Ben, describing his profession on the marriage certificate as a gent's mercer, settled with Lilian in Neath where, in 1921, they had their only daughter, Margaret.

In just a few short months, Cec had made a powerful impression on those who administered Army athletics. He remained stationed on Wimbledon Common for the rest of the year, a sporting asset spared a posting to the front which possibly saved his life; for certain it spared him much hardship and suffering in the hell of the trenches from which his peers had no escape. The last few months of the war saw the Queen's Westminster Rifles involved in some ferocious battles; the second Battles of the Somme and Arras, the Battles of the Hindenburg Line and the advance in Picardy

---

[*] Those silver cups have since been lost to time and circumstances, so the studio photograph of him posing with them are the only record of their existence.

where both sides suffered heavy losses in the desperate final struggle for supremacy.*

Moreover, his performances over established and famous military athletes had not gone unnoticed by those in high positions in the civilian sector of the sport, particularly the committee of the famous Surrey Athletic Club. Amongst their ranks were some of the best athletes in the land and their cumulative success as a club was practically unrivalled. The sight of one of their most respected members, Fred Mawby, being beaten by Cec in the 440 yards race at the Inter-Services Championship spurred them into action. Unbeknown to Cec, he was squarely in the sights of the powerful individual who ran the club. He was determined to elevate the young rifleman from being a military athlete to a level beyond his imagination.

* The majority of military service records appertaining to the First World War were destroyed by a fire caused by an incendiary bomb in London during the Blitz; many of the remaining papers display some degree of charring. It would be fascinating to know more about Cec's life with the QWR and see the reports from his superiors who made it possible for him to live in something of a bubble, protected from the reality of war because of his athletic gift.

Safely demobilised – at home in Neath
with mother, brother and sister

4

SUCCESS WITH SURREY
1919

By the spring of 1919, Cec had been demobbed from the Army. May was lucky that, as well as her boyfriend, all three of her brothers had defied the odds to survive the war. A year of army life had developed Cec's physique considerably. The relentless drills, marching, bayonet practise and nourishing food could not have been bettered as a training regime; for certain, Joe Binks never described him as frail again. Cec never carried much weight, but by the time he became a civilian he had more muscle to power his elegant, long strides around the race track.

On the back of international success in the military, Cec decided to continue as a competitive athlete. Several approaches from leading clubs eager to gain his membership made him realise he was hot property. The package offered by Surrey Athletic Club was the one that he chose – it had strong links with the military and already boasted several ex-servicemen amongst their talented members.

The chairman and founder of the club, E.F. 'Ted' Vowles, was an ambitious man who promised that Surrey would push Cec right to the top of the sport. No stranger to putting a few noses out of joint, Ted had renamed the club from Malden Harriers to Surrey AC in 1907, an attempt to portray the club as bigger and better compared to its local rivals. Ted gave Cec a job in his shirt factory in the East End of London and found lodgings for him at 44 Maryland Park, Stratford – in 2012, the site of Cec's bed was just over a mile from the finish line in the new Olympic Stadium. His landlady, Mrs Woodroffe, who had lost both husband and son during the war, became like a second mother to him, welcoming him into her home. Ted Vowles had two sons, Joe and Cyril, who became friends with Cec from the moment they met.

As Cec prepared for his new career in British athletics, the Amateur Athletic Association considered their position regarding the reinstatement of athletes as amateurs who had competed in professional events during the war. The New Zealand association had granted an amnesty to Dan Mason and governing bodies of athletics in other countries were following suit in the treatment of their Great War veterans.

It was a question that troubled the British association more than their international equivalents. The AAA was formed in 1880, instigated by senior officials of the Oxford University Athletic Club and backed by representatives of the major athletic clubs in the country. It took over as the governing body of the sport and one of its objectives was to make track and field athletics available to all classes of society. This was an admirable intention, but a difficult one to fulfil in practice. The rules governing amateurism – that athletes should not receive monetary recompense for competing – only allowed those with sufficient wealth to compete seriously in athletics. The idea that athletes should be paid to compete and become professionals was abhorrent.

As a result, there was little change in the status and class of athletes who competed under the AAA banner. The situation greatly favoured wealthy young men at university, especially Oxford and Cambridge, with plenty of time on their hands to learn their craft courtesy of their lax education timetables and plenty of resources courtesy of their parents' money. They competed against their social equals at other universities and the best went on to short national and international athletics careers prior to entering their chosen professions. The entry lists at major athletics events – as well as cricket, rowing and tennis – were dominated by university dons and were practically a closed shop for those from the lower classes of society. Many retired to become officials in their chosen sports, perpetuating the system and protecting the university old boy network.

The First World War began to break down these rigid barriers and promoted social mobility. Within the military, the class-based officer system simply could not cope with a shortage of suitable men to lead the troops and for the first time considerable numbers of men were promoted from the ranks to become officers. At the same time, a shortage of athletics meetings meant that amateurs were often forced to compete in professional events. The lines between us and them were beginning to blur.

Nevertheless, working-class men with inclinations to become an athlete during the 1920s were still trying to break into an alien and unwelcoming system. Athletes like Cec met with considerable difficulties; to compete and beat the established guard was an attack guaranteed to antagonise the proverbial feeding hand.

At the Annual General Meeting of the AAA on 12 April 1919, the following resolution was passed:

> Persons who have competed in amateur events prior to the war, but in Pro events during the war in the scarcity of AAA meetings in their District, should only be re-instated in special circumstances in the interests of those who have refrained from competing in Professional events.

The wording of this ruling was deliberately vague. It provided 'special circumstances' that could be considered in the decision-making process should a professional athlete want to rejoin the fold, but it did not define what those special circumstances were. It also fell some way short in establishing whether such a reinstated professional could compete internationally for Great Britain in the Olympic Games, at that stage the only international athletics contest between Britain and any other country.

With the AAA feeling that they had sufficiently dealt with the problem of wartime competition, it was time to return to normality. On 5 July 1919, Cec was able to turn out in the AAA Championship at Stamford Bridge, the first running of the event since 1914. With a capacity of 100,000, it was the second-largest ground in England after Crystal Palace and could accommodate the large sport-starved crowds eager to watch top-class athletics. It was a grand setting for Cec's first major event representing Surrey AC.

Having not previously belonged to a club and residing within twenty miles of Surrey AC's headquarters, Cec qualified as a first-claim member. To stop crack athletes frequently switching clubs and gathering together at one, the AAA had introduced a rule declaring:

> Each competitor in an open race must be a first-claim member of the club for which he is entered for three months prior to the event. If resident more than 20 miles from that club's headquarters, or entered by a club other than that which he last represented in an open team event, he must have been a first-claim member for 12 months prior to the competition.

An athlete could belong to another club if he wished but that would be his second-claim club, and although he could compete in that club's own closed events, he could not take part in open inter-club, inter-team or relay races as part of a scoring team under AAA laws for his second-claim club. However, club chairmen and presidents soon became adept at manipulating and circumnavigating the rules to attract the best athletes to their particular organisation.

Low cloud hung over London as the excited crowd, numbering 15,000, poured into the stadium to watch the championship event. Some 5,000 packed into the stand on the east side and the rest, despite the threatened rain, filled the exposed terraces. To their relief, and that of the competitors, the rain stayed away and an international field of athletes keenly contested a full programme of field and track events. At the AAA Championship – which was effectively the British Championship – it was customary for the AAA to invite top competitors from foreign clubs to add variety and draw in the crowds. This occasion was no exception and there was a large contingent from Sweden, Norway and Denmark. New Zealand was also well represented, likely because many of their athletes were still serving on the continent. The passage of time and the impact of war had severely affected the entry lists. Only a few athletes had competed in the previous AAA Championship in 1914, and only two men were on hand to defend their titles.

At nineteen and a half, Cec was still classified as a junior. For one so young to be pitted against some of the best athletes in the world was a daunting prospect, but competing at Stamford Bridge twice before for the military must have helped him steady his nerves in front of such a large, enthusiastic audience.

Still relatively unknown outside of military circles, not many would have been expecting Cec to progress through the heats to take his place on the line for the final of the 440 yards. Yet he did so, and in a fast final, timed at 49.8,

Cec came third, two yards behind the winner. Guy Butler (Cambridge University AC) took the title, with Nils Engdahl (Sweden) second and Bevil Rudd (Oxford University AC) fourth. The careers of the four runners would overlap for some years, but this was the first time the stylish runner from a working-class community in Neath, without the benefit of a university education, would take on the might of the established Oxbridge old school.

Nor was he the only working-class athlete who was taking on the old guard. William Hill and Albert Hill, two athletes who shared a surname but were not related, had no affiliations with any university athletic club and were not part of the privileged elite. William had come into athletics through the military, having served in the Royal Field Artillery and, like Cec, had only been discharged three months before the Championship to join Surrey AC. His first AAA titles in the 100 and 220 yards sprints on the soft track were exceptional performances and a declaration of his arrival in the sport.

Albert Hill, on the other hand, was no stranger to athletics. He was the 1910 AAA four mile champion and runner up in the 1914 AAA half mile. Service with the Royal Flying Corps had interrupted his career and, at 30 years of age, most had written him off as a serious contender in the 1919 Championship. His victories in the half mile, mile and relay were the highlights of the meeting; it would not be the last time he would prove his doubters wrong

During the war, the military used sport as a means to prepare men for conflict and to boost morale. In the aftermath of war, it was a decisive factor in uniting nations who fought together and against each other. Nevertheless, there were barriers to international competition.

In the summer of 1919, it was decided to hold a multi-sport event, the Inter-Allied Games, at the Pershing Stadium in Paris. The competition was designed for military personnel who were currently serving or had served in the armed forces during the war. Cec would have been eligible to compete but several countries, including Great Britain, declined to send an official team to the two-week event. The AAA scheduled their championship so that it clashed with the military competition. It was an indication of the British attitude towards immediate post-war contests – they felt that they lacked the ability to organise and fund international competition while the country was still recovering from war. Poverty and hardship were rife; unemployment and high taxes were crippling the economy. David Lloyd George's Liberal Party would have feared the reaction from their voters if public money was spent in a way perceived to be frivolous.

That didn't stop eighteen of their former allies. The USA was heavily involved, the prime mover in the organisation of the Inter-Allied Games. The American military constructed the stadium and gifted it to France. Dan Mason, the professional New Zealand athlete who Cec had surprisingly beaten in 1918, won the 800 metres. Later in the year he returned home where the New Zealand AAA amnesty allowed him to resume his amateur career.

The reaction of the British authorities to the Inter-Allied Games matched their attitude to the resurrection of the Olympic Games. This had been announced by the International Olympic Committee on 5 April 1919, when they awarded the seventh Olympic Games to Antwerp, in recognition of Belgium's bravery during the war. This immediately sparked a debate in the UK concerning the nation's ability to prepare an Olympic team within a year. Even at the very time British athletes were competing at Stamford Bridge and their international colleagues were on display in the Pershing Stadium, the Olympic debate raged in the letters pages of *The Times*.

The British Olympic team – Cec is standing with a hand
on Percy Hodge's shoulder

5

THE YEAR OF THE
OLYMPIAD
1920

Only Australia, Great Britain and Greece can boast that their athletes have appeared at every modern Olympic Games. In the middle of August 1920, 39 British athletes were sent on their way to contribute to that sporting history. Cec was among them. He was probably in a state of nervous excitement in anticipation of his first trip outside the United Kingdom to represent his country. What he didn't realise was that it was a trip that very nearly didn't happen. Only the 1980 Moscow Olympics can come close to matching the upheaval the British Olympic Association had to overcome in 1920.

The Olympic Games scheduled for 1920 gave participating countries precious little time to prepare their national teams and some serious issues to discuss. First was the question as to whether Germany should be allowed to compete. Baron Pierre de Coubertin, the father of the modern Olympic Games, allegedly made a statement in February 1915 emphasising the International Olympic Committee's neutrality during the war and that Germany should keep the right to host the gathering in 1916. The continuation of the war meant that the Berlin Olympics were never likely to take place and de Coubertin later denied making the statement, but not before the outcry led to the resignation of influential members of the IOC including Britain's Sir Theodore Andrea Cook.

The dilemma remained in 1920. The IOC fudged a diplomatic solution which allowed the organising committee of the host country to send out the invitations to compete. The IOC then simply turned a blind eye when the Belgian committee did not send invitations to the defeated powers; Germany, Austria, Hungary, Bulgaria and Turkey. This was extended to Bolshevik Russia, embroiled in revolution, who were unlikely to have sent a team anyway.*

* When the French committee sent out their invitations for the 1924 Paris Olympics, they continued to exclude Germany, which was not surprising considering France's suffering in the war. Athletes from Austria, Hungary and Turkey were welcomed back into the fold.

Of course, just because a country had been invited, it did not mean that they had to compete. The British athletics authorities had chosen not to send athletes to the Inter-Allied Games and there was a strong argument in favour of declining the Olympic invitation too.

The working man felt no affiliation with the Olympic Games. There was no incentive for him to attend, let alone compete, and he would have considered the British Olympic Association to be elitist, administered by the aristocracy who favoured their own athletes from Oxford and Cambridge. To a great extent, he would have been right – the entire track and field team at the previous 1912 Olympics in Stockholm comprised of Oxbridge Blues. Mass support for sporting events was mainly reserved for football, although cricket, rugby, cycling, boxing and horse racing could also draw large crowds. The activities of mostly foreign runners, jumpers and throwers in a distant Olympic stadium held no attraction whatsoever for most people. Theodore Cook, who had resigned from the IOC in the wake of de Coubertin's comments about Germany, captured the mood of the nation when he wrote, 'The truth is that the average Englishman would far rather see Oxford beat Cambridge, or Surrey fighting Yorkshire... than any amount of Czechoslovakians squaring up to a South American Republic.'

Surprisingly, there was also minimal support from the upper and middle classes. They considered the Olympics a derisory, political invention; the brainchild of de Coubertin, a suspiciously French-led affair. They preferred to associate themselves with quintessentially English events such as tennis at Wimbledon, cricket at Lord's or rowing at Henley.

A typical attitude was that displayed by political reformer Frederick Harrison, who declared, 'They may be Olympic, but they are not English. It is not "cricket", as we used to play it at Oxford in the fifties.'

The BOA, whose responsibility it was to arrange for the British team of athletes to attend the Olympic Games and once there to oversee the essential necessities of transport, food and accommodation, was practically bankrupt following the suspension of subscriptions during the war and the loss of many leading members in the conflict. Just over a week after the IOC met in Lausanne to award the 1920 Games to Antwerp, the BOA made a patriotic appeal in *The Times* for the public to support the Games. They set a target of £30,000, but by the time the Olympics rolled round, only a fifth of that had been acquired. There were many other appeals competing for charitable donations; communities wanted money for war memorials and there was widespread demand for hospitals to care for the wounded war veterans, while the Spanish influenza had added to the grim toll of the war and taken away yet more breadwinners.

Following the BOA appeal, *The Times* published a letter from two Stockholm Olympians – Arnold Strode-Jackson, who won the 1,500 metres, and Philip Noel-Baker, who had been a finalist in the same event. Each had been decorated in wartime. Strode-Jackson was a conventional soldier who was rewarded for bravery, Noel-Baker was a pacifist and devout Quaker who set up and led the Friends Ambulance Unit throughout the slaughter in Europe, and received medals from Britain, Italy and France for his humanitarian work.[*] Both veterans demanded the Olympic Games be postponed for two years to allow the participating nations to recover. They were horrified to discover the state that the war had left most of the prestigious athletic clubs in and considered the cost of sending athletes abroad could be put to better use.

The Government was equally unwilling to contribute. Poverty was rife. The national debt had increased to an unimaginable level. Recession was making unemployment soar. There were troubles in Ireland following the declaration of the Irish Republic in January 1919. The Russian Revolution had financial and political implications.

The odds were stacked heavily against the BOA and it was unlikely that the Olympic invitation was going to be received favourably. That it was accepted came down to a quirk of fate and the initiative of Ernest Lebuman, an official nearing retirement in the foreign office.

The invitation reached its destination in October 1919. As was usual, it was delivered to the Foreign Office in Whitehall. Lebuman should have forwarded it to the BOA for consideration, especially in view of the controversy surrounding the Olympics. Instead, he took it upon himself to formally accept the invitation on behalf of the nation. His actions flew in the face of overwhelming opposition and apathy. It is most likely the BOA would have politely refused to take part in view of the derisory amount of money its appeal had

---

[*] Noel-Baker continued his humanitarian work in later life, being involved with the formation of the League of Nations and the United Nations during his career as a diplomat and politician. He campaigned for multilateral nuclear disarmament and won the Nobel Peace Prize in 1952 – the only Nobel Laureate to have won an Olympic medal.

raised and the pressure from a government concerned with losing votes if they funded it.

However, they were hamstrung by the actions of a single bureaucrat and could not withdraw without losing face. From the moment the BOA was informed that an error by the Foreign Office had committed Britain to be represented at Antwerp, the objectors – Arnold Strode-Jackson, Philip Noel-Baker and Theodore Cook among them – put their doubts aside and became leading figures in supporting the campaign.

Professional fundraisers were employed but made little difference. By June 1920, just two months before the opening ceremony, only £1,800 had been raised. King George had donated £100 and some politicians, including Secretary of State for War, Winston Churchill, had personally given more, but the Government steadfastly refused to commit funds, even though their error had brought about the predicament. Other foreign governments, like those of the USA and France, were providing for their Olympic teams, but the British allowed senior officials to issue statements of negativity condemning the Games. 'The Olympic Games are an international farce,' declared Sir Eyre Crowe, Assistant Under-Secretary for Foreign Affairs, the government department that had inadvertently accepted the invitation to attend and then denied any funding.

While officialdom bothered itself with the issue of whether Britain should compete, athletes like Cec were more bothered about putting themselves in the frame for selection in case Britain did compete. Cec made significant strides towards Antwerp when he won a silver medal depicting an ancient Olympiad scene which was simply engraved 'AAA Olympic Trials 1920', but there is no date or venue associated with it and its origins remains unknown.

The Northern, Midland and Southern Olympic Trial meetings were all held on or prior to 12 June and the AAA made available sets of specially designed gold, silver and bronze medals for scratch Olympic open events. Cec's medal could not have come from the Southern Olympic Trial meeting held at Stamford Bridge on 12 June, because the first two runners in the 440 yards were Scotland's Robert Lindsay and H.R. Wicks.*

Following the trials, the AAA Special Olympic Committee met at their London offices in Piccadilly on 14 June, just two days after the deadline set for holding the trials. Seven athletes were invited to continue with their training for the Olympic 400 metres. Cec was not among them, and there is no mention of him anywhere in the documents. Cec believed that the AAA, in particular the Honorary Secretary, Harry Barclay, considered him too young and working class to compete on the grandest of stages. Instead of taking note of his outstanding achievements as a junior, they chose to ignore him and look towards the more established athletes.

Cec was not the only athlete who was disgruntled by the AAA in the run up to the Olympic Games. Albert Hill, whose three wins on the same day in the 1919 AAA Championship had brought about the event to be split over two days, was similarly disillusioned by authority. Hill should

---

* Although the Olympic events were held over metric distances (100 metres, 200 metres, 400 metres...) the AAA had decided to retain imperial measurement of race distances for Olympic trials and the AAA Championship (100 yards, 220 yards, 440 yards...) which persisted until metrication was adopted in 1969.

have been a first choice for the Olympic team, but he shared a similar working-class background to Cec and had to overcome the class prejudices and barriers put up by those who governed their sport.

Albert did not attend the trials on principle due to a long-running dispute about the AAA's treatment of him. Since the war, his athletics performances had event promoters clamouring for his participation. To make races more interesting, especially in the south of the country, some officials made Albert owe a distance, forcing him to start behind the scratch mark. This was based on a misinterpretation of the AAA rule which levied an eight-yard penalty on any athlete in a handicap race who had previously won first prize in such a race. The AAA rule stated that penalties should not be enforced beyond the scratch mark, stopping top runners being made to run a longer distance. Albert's argument was reasonable – if he entered an 880 yards race, he didn't expect to run 888 yards. Aside from making it harder to win, it would make breaking any records nigh impossible. He blamed this repeated breach of regulations on southern region AAA officials and focused on competitions in the north and midlands, where the officials tended to apply the laws correctly.

The AAA, who Albert described as 'dictators', reacted by launching an investigation into his status as an amateur, delving into the value of prizes he had received and how he financed his travelling to the north. It was a low blow – they were threatening Albert's ability to compete in any competition at all. Harry Barclay was the workhorse of the AAA investigations. He travelled widely, not just to athletics events but also to visit athletes at their homes and interrogate them about their finances.

Barclay's investigations into Albert demonstrated just how far he was removed from the lives of his working-class athletes. An official with any common sense should have been aware that, as an employee of a railway company, Albert would be entitled to free train travel. The last straw came when Barclay paid a surprise visit to his place of work demanding an immediate answer as to whether he would compete in a forthcoming international meeting. Barclay became angry and agitated when Albert told him he would have to wait until his bosses authorised his leave. Their confrontation ended with Albert refusing to take part in future events, including the forthcoming Olympic trials, knowing it would preclude him from going to Antwerp.

The AAA was not prepared to throw away one of its best medal hopes, so despite not attending the trials, Albert was informed by Barclay that he had been entered for the Olympic 800 metres. Yet although they considered he was a medal contender, they thought he was too old at 31 to also contest the 1,500 metres. Nevertheless, in a series of acrimonious meetings with Barclay, the forceful Albert managed to convince him of his abilities to tackle both events. If he was going to run in the Olympics, he wanted to run in both races.

With a provisional team announced – missing Cec – the AAA Championship took place at Stamford Bridge on 3 July. In the country's most prestigious 440 yards race, Cec came third for the second consecutive year. It was something that the selectors could not ignore. The winner of the race, Bevil Rudd, was eligible to compete for either his native

South Africa or for Great Britain by virtue of his scholarship to Oxford University. He chose the country of his birth, eliminating himself from the list of British runners available for selection in the 400 metres. Guy Butler came second, booking his place for the Olympic contest, just six weeks away. The rest of the team was unclear.

The AAA Special Olympic Committee met again, on 6 July 1920, to make a further provisional selection for the British team. This time, Cec was included in the list for the 400 metres. His performance the previous weekend spoke louder than words and left them with no room to reasonably exclude him. They still had one more opportunity to consider their options before making a final decision.

The inaugural Triangular International Contest between England, Scotland and Ireland (Wales counted as part of the English team until 1948) was held in 1914, just three weeks before Europe's descent into chaos and oblivion. In 1920, it was decided to revive the contest. The country's best athletes decamped to Crewe on 10 July, with Cec among them in the English team.

Once again, Cec came third. Bevil Rudd was the victor with Hedges Worthington-Eyre in second place. The overall result of the contest was nearly identical to that of 1914, with England dominating – hardly surprising given the difference in populations. Cec's international debut provided the selectors with one last chance to assess the potential Olympic team.

The AAA immediately sent out letters of invitation and within two weeks, once they had received all replies, they announced the British team for the Games. Having silenced his critics on the committees, Cec was selected for the individual 400 metres and the 4x400 metres relay. Worthington-Eyre also joined him on the basis of his results at Crewe – unlike Cec, he hadn't even been included in the second provisional selection. Guy Butler and Robert Lindsay completed the relay team which was backed up by two reserves, Jack Ainsworth-Davis and Dennis Bullough. The cast for the drama which would soon unfold had been set.

The fiercely patriotic Welsh press seized upon the news that one of their sons was going to Antwerp and headlines such as 'Neath sprinter for Olympic Games' in the *South Wales Daily News* proudly proclaimed his achievement. Two weeks ahead of his departure for Belgium, Cec could see the depth of Welsh pride for himself – he returned to Neath on 27 July 1920 for the wedding of his sister Eva to Rees Harris at St David's Church.

Cec would have enjoyed being at home in the bosom of his family, especially with May at his side. Either the alcohol or his recent athletic successes must have intoxicated his emotions, prompting him to declare his deep love and his intention to marry her. For a man known to keep his innermost feelings under control, this was a rare display of passion and probably the nearest May got to a formal proposal of marriage.

On 11 August 1920, because of the dogged perseverance of a few individuals, Cec and his 38 poorly-funded teammates boarded the boat for the short trip to Antwerp. They would have felt fortunate to be representing their country and the rough Channel crossing would not have deterred them. They had all been blessed with a gift, a natural talent which elevated them above their peers, and each of them had survived four years of war. But they were unaware of the single most determining factor in their collective fortune – a mistake by Ernest Lebuman in the Foreign Office.

Veteran medallists – Philip Noel-Baker and Albert Hill

6

ALBERT'S
DOUBLE
AUGUST 1920

A delegation of AAA executives travelled one day ahead of the athletes to meet with other national athletics associations and inspect the accommodation and facilities secured by the BOA for the British team. At the communal school lent by the Belgian authorities, where the athletes would sleep and eat, they discovered extremely bare rooms. The bedding supplied by the Belgian Red Cross left a good deal to be desired.

They were also unhappy with the position of the lavatory so close to the kitchen and made a protest to the authorities, but they must have known it was futile. There was no time to find alternative accommodation and the BOA had done their best with the funds available.

The British tug of war team, comprised of eight London policemen, was billeted in the same school as the athletes. They must have suffered a poor first night's sleep as their bunks collapsed, one by one, under the weight of the heavy men. A personal diary written by Hendrikus Alexander Janssen, one of the second-placed Dutch team, recorded that the British, who unsurprisingly won the event, were in total 300 kilograms heavier than his team. They remain the reigning champions as the event was removed from the Olympic schedule after Antwerp. The organisers probably couldn't afford their food bills.

The delegation reported that 'the athletes fell in with what was provided in a sporting spirit' and praised one of their own, team manager and AAA member, Colonel Kentish CMG DSO. Apart from maintaining high morale, he had taken advantage of his military contacts to procure trucks and an ambulance to transport the British team around Antwerp, which was essential in view of their precarious finances. The rough cobbled roads made the three miles from the school to the stadium an uncomfortable journey for the athletes sitting on makeshift wooden benches in the back of the vehicles. This was not ideal, especially after a hurried meal, so Colonel Kentish did his best to arrange cars for athletes who were due to perform that day; a privilege taken for granted by other teams.

Relaxation was assisted by a military band and musical evenings were hosted to which friends and athletes from other countries were encouraged to visit. For a few, including Cec, it was their first time abroad and the experience of attempting to communicate in a plethora of different languages with like-minded men was challenging and fulfilling. Not all the competing athletes would be rewarded with a medal, but everybody would cherish happy memories and new friendships were forged.

Albert Hill had been to Belgium twice before. The first time was in 1912 where he won two major international races in Brussels, for which he received two marble busts and a problem carrying them back to England along with his luggage. The second time was four years later to defend Ypres during the war, which presented him with substantially greater discomforts and difficulties getting home.

Belgium was slowly recovering from the ravages of conflict. Much of the country was still devastated; amenities were basic and woefully inadequate for the massive influx of Olympic visitors. More than 2,500 men and 65 women competing for 29 countries in 22 sports were crammed into Antwerp, creating a great deal of extra burden and pressure on the city's infrastructure. The administrative costs for the host country led to the bankruptcy of the organising committee. This compounded the logistical problems facing competitors and officials alike and was the reason why there was never an official 1920 Olympic Games report. Only a few individually-typed unofficial copies were produced which are now very scarce.

Water had to be boiled before consumption. Having been ill in the war from drinking the Ypres water, Albert Hill took no risks and existed on a diet of local beer, while the American team were savvy enough to organise their own supply of bottled water. Albert threatened to withdraw if the standard of food wasn't improved and in protest breakfasted at a local hotel, presenting the bill for payment to an incensed Harry Barclay.

The stadium of the Royal Beerschot Athletic Club had undergone a facelift which cost the city well in excess of two million Belgian Francs. In some areas, it still resembled a building site. Percy Hodge, Britain's sole steeplechaser and favourite to win the 3,000 metres race, must have been shocked when he saw the water jump with its steep, muddy sides and deep water. It resembled a stinking trench from the battlefront – hardly surprising, considering that the Belgian Army had constructed many of the facilities in great haste.

A photograph taken of the British, Canadian and South African teams assembled on the terraces beside the track inadvertently captured a grim image of that water jump. The group of over 300 meant that the anonymous snapper had to move far into the infield to get them all in the frame and the intimidating jump dominates the foreground. The athletes are so far away that individuals can only be identified under magnification, but Cec can be made out standing beside Albert Hill.

A similar photograph shows the British athletics team posing for an official portrait, all dressed in their immaculate white strip with the Union Jack emblazoned on the chest. Most of the men look stern, a few confident faces are smiling. Cec has placed a reassuring hand on the shoulder of Percy Hodge in front of him.

Despite the extensive and expensive renovation of the Beerschot Stadium, the track was not modified to convert it to the internationally recognised length of 400 metres. At 389.8 metres, it provided a headache for the officials who had to determine how many laps, or parts of laps, had to be completed for specific distances, especially in the longer races. The first qualifying heat of the men's ten kilometres walk, won by Ugo Frigerio of Italy, was miscalculated and only 9,610 metres were covered. Luckily it made no difference to the results as Frigerio was a class above his competitors. Immediately prior to the final he handed out sheet music to the band to be played during the race and at one point stopped to show them the correct tempo, before continuing to win by more than 90 seconds.

Considering that Belgium had emerged from the war with a near-collapsed economy, it was indulgent that the railway had been extended from Antwerp Gare Centrale to a new station built beside the stadium. With a fine sense of occasion, the first train carried King Albert, Queen Elizabeth and their three children to the lavish opening ceremony on 14 August. There, the seventh Olympiad was formally opened by the king watched by a crowd of 20,000.

The Parade of Nations was a colourful spectacle in bright sunlight. Competitors from each country, nation by nation, led by a flag bearer, marched before the royal box and around the arena to line up facing His Majesty. Photographs of the British team in their ill-fitting uniforms of light grey flannel trousers and blue blazer topped off with a straw boater indicate the tight budget they were on. The clothes were certainly not bespoke. Some of the blazers hung like sacks over their shoulders. For those with a fuller figure, the buttons were strained; and the trousers of tall athletes were several inches above their ankles.

The colourful, striking national costumes caught the eye of the reporter for the *Hull Daily Mail*. He described the Egyptian's sober black coats and red fezzes, the muscular shoulders of the Greeks in their sleeveless jerseys, the turbans of British India and the French with red Gallic cocks embroidered on their chests, but it was the Scandinavian representatives he found most endearing: 'Perhaps the most engaging features of the procession were two bands of fair-haired maidens in close-fitting bright blue garments marching under the flags of Denmark and Sweden.'

After the king formally declared the Games open, three new innovations were introduced. The Olympic flag, designed in 1912 by Baron Pierre de Coubertin, was raised to a trumpet fanfare. Then, poignantly, doves were released to symbolise peace. Lastly, the athlete's oath was taken. This was written by de Coubertin and taken by an athlete of the host nation, on behalf of all athletes, while holding a corner of the Olympic flag. At Antwerp, fencer Victor Boin became the first to utter the words:

> In the name of all competitors, I promise that we shall take part in these Olympic Games, respecting and abiding by the rules that govern them, in the true spirit of sportsmanship, for the glory of sport and the honour of our teams.

This concluded the successful opening ceremony but heralded a frantic surge of activity by contractors to ready the stadium for the commencement of the athletics the next day.

By special telegram, King George V sent a special message to all competitors of the British Empire:

> I send you all who are upholding the reputation of the British Empire in the Olympic Games my best wishes for your success and good luck. I know that whether victorious or defeated in the various contests, you will exercise an inspiring influence in promoting the spirit of competition. You can rest assured that your every achievement and daily progress will be followed by me with the closest interest and keenness.

One of the first of those athletes who the king would be monitoring was Albert Hill. His Olympic debut commenced in the 800 metres on Sunday 15 August, the first day of competition. It was certainly not a day of rest – there was some discontent voiced when Albert saw the programme and discovered the Belgian officials had placed the top three contenders for the Olympic title in the same heat. Albert, Bevil Rudd and Earl Eby were all placed in the second of five heats, with only the top four in each race to qualify. When questioned, the organisers explained that they thought this was the normal procedure in order to give other competitors a chance. They could not change it as the programme had been published. As it turned out, all three progressed through to the semi-finals. So too did another British runner in a different heat, nineteen-year-old Edgar Mountain of Cambridge University AC. On 17 August, the four of them took their place in the final.

Albert was an experienced runner and made full use of it to plan his race strategy. He knew American Eby would go off at a fast pace and that South African Rudd would prefer to track him closely before making a big effort near the finish. Albert kept well back until the bell. Then he surged past Eby to take the lead, anticipating a fight back from Rudd who swept by him with half a lap to go. Entering the home straight, Rudd extended his lead to three metres. Most thought he was on his way to victory, but Albert noticed the leader's rhythm and balance was disintegrating and summoned every last effort to catch him. Eby, also realising that Rudd was fading, went with Albert. Both overwhelmed Rudd with just yards to go but it was Albert, his leg swathed in flapping bandages, who inched into the lead to win by 0.2 seconds. Rudd collapsed on the soft track at the finish, having been forced to sprint too early by Albert's move.

Amongst all of Albert's many contests he considered it stood out as 'the victory based most satisfyingly on judgement and tactics'. He had won Britain's first gold medal for eight years, and had Rudd chosen to run for Britain rather than South Africa, there could have been two British medallists on the podium. Young Edgar Mountain was a creditable fourth and his time of 1:54.6 was a new best junior time. Hill was in the twilight of his career and Mountain made a clear statement of intent that he wanted to be the future of the British half mile.

On 18 August, just a day after the punishing 800 metres final, Albert and two other British competitors, team captain Philip Noel-Baker and Scot Duncan McPhee, came second in their respective 1,500 metres heats to qualify for the next day's final.

That evening, Cec and Albert spent some time together. They already got on well and had much in common. Both shared a working-class background and had to train themselves. Albert had gone on long distance runs in his youth and would have envied Cec's runs along the towpath in the wide green valleys and rolling hills of South Wales. Albert recalled nightly runs along Drury Lane, when bored youngsters, hanging around the street corners, hurled rotten fruit and abuse at him. Since then, Albert had joined Polytechnic Harriers and used the wisdom of the club coach, Sam Mussabini, to aid his performances. Mussabini's professional coaching status was controversial but there was no doubt about his ability. He had successfully coached professional cyclists before he became involved with athletics and had coached gold medal winners at the 1908 and 1912 Olympics.

Cec and Albert also shared an achievement that they alone could claim – they were the only runners to have beaten Dan Mason during his wartime service. Cec did it first, in the 440 yards at the Inter-Services Championship. Albert claimed his scalp in a half mile race in 1919. Both also had a common enemy, feeling that Harry Barclay of the AAA had unfairly targeted them – Cec in terms of his Olympic selection, Albert in terms of suspicions of professionalism over his expenses and travel costs.

A note on one of Cec's postcards brings to light an intriguing conversation which mentions the tantalising possibility that their paths may have crossed as early as 1915:

> Chatted to Albert Hill on the evening before our races just before I was ill. Told me he loves Wales, and on a visit to Merthyr Tydfil before he went to war had seen some boys racing near there from the train. Could have been me!

It is just about feasible he was correct. In 1915, the year we know Cec was racing at the Great September Fair, Albert was undergoing Royal Flying Corps training in Farnborough. It is conceivable he visited his uncle in Wales to proudly show off his new uniform before his posting to the Western Front. The precise dates of Albert's leave are unknown, but at worst Albert passed only a few miles from Cec and there were few races in South Wales during 1915. It must have been frustrating for Albert to see the youngsters, knowing his own career in athletics had been halted by the war; mercifully he had no idea that it would last for three more murderous years. It is a delicious concept to imagine the veteran and boy athletes being brought together by mysterious fate, five years in advance of their shared adventure in Antwerp.

Albert was renowned for his ability to relax in the build up to a race, and he must have been looking forward to his second Olympic final, already a gold medallist. Cec's stomach was churning. It was the evening before his own Olympic debut in the heats of the 400 metres. However, it was not just nerves getting to him. After suffering a miserable night of gripping stomach pains and sickness, he was taken to the infirmary, a victim of the insanitary conditions or infected water. He was declared too ill to compete. Perhaps the lavatory close to the kitchen was the thing that scuppered Cec's Olympic debut.

Albert's second Olympic final did not match the suspense of the 800 metres. Fearing the American contingent, he deployed exactly the same tactics and won the race comfortably. McPhee retired, but the most excitement of the race was provided by Philip Noel-Baker, veteran of the 1,500 metres at Stockholm, who shadowed Albert to take an inspired second place and silver medal. No medal was more deserved considering the efforts he had made to assemble an underfunded team. He had put his personal opinions aside because his country needed him and received his just reward.

Albert was carried triumphantly on the shoulders of the crowd and was congratulated by King Albert on his magnificent performance. It was as if Belgium, with half of her towns still in ruin, was thanking him for his part in her defence and repaying its debt of gratitude to a soldier who had fought so hard to defend Ypres.*

Cec was too ill to watch, let alone run in the heats of the 400 metres. His slot was given to one of the reserves, Jack Ainsworth-Davis, Cec's fellow countryman from Aberystwyth. He had served as a captain in the Rifle Brigade, then a pilot in Egypt with the RFC during the war. When peace came he went to Christ's College, Cambridge where at the age of nearly 25 his late involvement in national athletics commenced.

---

* The 800/1,500 metres Olympic double has not been achieved by a British male since, although Kelly Holmes won both women's events at Athens in 2004. It was not until Mo Farah won 5,000 and 10,000 metres at London in 2012 that another British male track and field athlete won double Olympic titles.

The fact that Ainsworth-Davis was in the Olympic team at all was remarkable considering that he had achieved so little in domestic championships. Perhaps the fact that he was Guy Butler's Cambridge University AC teammate had something to do with it. Nevertheless, fate had dealt Ainsworth-Davis a lucky opportunity to compete at the highest level. Cec was on the receiving end.

British runners Ainsworth-Davis, Butler, Robert Lindsay and Hedges Worthington-Eyre, all in separate heats, qualified for the afternoon's quarter-finals, but only the two Cambridge men went through to the next day's semi-finals, one in each race. It seemed that Worthington-Eyre had peaked too early in the year when he won the 440 yards at the Irish AAA Championship and beat Cec for second place in the Triangular International Contest.

The following day, Cec was over the worst of his illness and watched his replacement, Ainsworth-Davis, come third in his semi-final in which all three qualifiers broke the 50-second barrier for the first time in the competition. Butler finished second in his semi-final. The final, which was held just over two hours later, was incredibly close. Bevil Rudd crossed the line first in 49.6 to become the 400 metres Olympic Champion. The next three runners finished in a dead heat on 49.9. The atmosphere was tense as the officials deliberated their decision. They eventually awarded second place to Butler, with Nils Engdahl of Sweden third. Ainsworth-Davis was the next finisher behind the dead heat with 50.0.

Cec knew he would have had a chance to take home a medal if fate had not been so cruel. He could have matched his performances in the previous two AAA Championships and got on the podium – and in such a close contest, he could have even made it to the top step.

Earlier in the day, Percy Hodge had overcome the muddy water jump to win the 3,000 metres steeplechase in a new Olympic record and earn the third gold medal for Great Britain. The shoemaker's son from Guernsey had triumphed in the event that he was expected to win. Another ten track and field events remained over the next three days, and the expectations of adding to the medal tally placed the competitors under a great deal of pressure. Cec had one more chance to make a contribution to his country's Olympic effort. Could he get back to full fitness to perform at the level he was capable of?

The victorious relay team: Guy Butler, Jack Ainsworth-Davis, Robert Lindsay and Cecil Griffiths

7

OLYMPIC

GLORY

AUGUST 1920

Cec had until 10.50 on the morning of Sunday 22 August, when the first heat of the 4x400 metres relay was scheduled, to prove his fitness.

The extra two days since the 400 metres final had given Cec time to rest, but although he was feeling much better, more than three days of sickness had sapped his energy, jeopardising his chance to make the team. Illness could mean that he would travel to Antwerp and watch the entire Olympics from the stands.

Guy Butler's speed and 30-year-old Robert Lindsay's experience made them undoubted choices. Jack Ainsworth-Davis pushed his way into the team on the back of his surprisingly impressive performance to finish fifth in the 400 metres. That left one remaining place and three men desperate to secure it; Dennis Bullough, Hedges Worthington-Eyre and Cec.

The final decision rested with the team captain, Philip Noel-Baker with input from his vice-captain, Victor d'Arcy. They were both experienced veterans of the 1912 Olympics; d'Arcy had won a gold medal in the sprint relay so his advice was particularly valuable. They recognised that Cec, even if not at his best, was still the strongest candidate based on his form and consistency over the past year. Moreover, his health had improved considerably since he became ill. Yet they still showed great faith in naming Cec in the team for the heats because the rules stated that the team could not be altered between the heat and final. If Cec performed badly in the heat, they would still have to include him in the final.

Great Britain's track and field athletes had not added any more gold medals to the ones won by Albert Hill and Percy Hodge, so hopes and expectations were higher than ever. Cec and his teammates were due to run in the first of the two heats, three teams in each, which were listed in the programme as semi-finals. Only six countries had entered this event, so providing each team ran within the rules they were guaranteed a place in the final to be held the following day to battle it out for the medals. Cec was tasked with running the first leg, laying a solid foundation for the rest of the team. Normal practice was to put the best runner last and the second-best runner first, so there was a lot of pressure resting on Cec's shoulders.

Belgium, Britain and France were in the first heat; South Africa, USA and Sweden in the second. The pace of both heats, even allowing for the slow track, was sedate. The only competitive aspect related to the lane draw for the final, but even that was of little concern as the start was in a line on the straight rather than staggered on the bend. The priority was to not make a mistake and qualify.

The South African team set the fastest time of 3:38.6. The British team came second in their heat in 3:40.9, a time that was fourth-fastest overall. Both were a long way from the world and Olympic record of 3:16.6 set by the American team at Stockholm in 1912, but there was never any likelihood of it being broken on the slow Antwerp track.

Shortly after the relay, Albert Hill helped Joe Blewitt, William Seagrove and James Hatton secure a silver medal for Great Britain in the 3,000 metres team race with USA taking gold. Three medals, two gold, from seven races in eight days. Albert Hill had secured his place in history and proven that he was right to stand up to Harry Barclay over entering multiple events.

Adrenaline had seen Cec through the first round, watched by the biggest crowd he had ever performed in front of. He still felt a little sick and he found it difficult to relax leading up to the final. He occupied himself by filling his autograph book with the signatures of Olympians from several sports, meeting some famous personalities in the process.

The 4x400 metres relay on Monday 23 August was the last event on the final day of athletics competition. Cec knew that he had to maintain his composure and keep his nerves under control until the 3 o'clock start if he wanted to achieve a fast and faultless lap on the loose track. Wasting nervous energy could only set him back. Although Bevil Rudd's South Africans were the favourites to win, hopes were high for the British team that included the second and fifth placed finishers in the individual event.

When he entered the stadium, Cec was captivated by the noise of the animated crowd of 29,000 who were close to the track. Most of the mainly male audience was immaculately dressed in suit, tie and boater. Many of the straw hats were being waved. Cec could hear distinctly British accents cheering. There were many British subjects living and working in Belgium, many of whom had generously donated to their home country's Olympic appeal.

The brash American cheerleader could not be missed. This fine man (female cheerleaders would not be introduced until 1923) led the crowd and was a novel experience for the European spectators. Compared in *All Sports Weekly* to a conductor in an orchestra, he had singled out Albert Hill's fine performances for his enthusiastic attention. The American spectators were very fair and never failed to cheer a British winner.

Cec's fear of failure while representing his country at the highest level was almost crushing. There are many variables in a relay, any one of which can go wrong and spell disaster. The British team decided to not change the tried and tested formula from the semi-final and ran in the same order. Cec would start in lane four with the South African, Belgian and American runners to his left and those from Sweden and France to his right. Once he had relinquished the baton, fate would be out of his hands. It was down to Lindsay, Ainsworth-Davis and Butler to carry it safely to the finishing line ahead of the twenty men in five other teams.

As Cec took his mark for the last event in the stadium, the high spirits of the crowd lifted him. He relaxed his white-knuckle grip on the bamboo baton which had to be carried safely for one mile to the finishing tape by the four of them in turn. The start was at the top of the home straight and each subsequent handover point was a further ten metres down the straight to compensate for the 390-metre track. Cec had kicked holes in the soft cinders to give himself purchase when he pushed off. As he waited for the starter's signal, he crouched forward over the line. He was the only one holding the baton in his right hand, presumably to facilitate the change to left-handed Lindsay; he didn't want to risk changing hands mid-run. His senses would have been on high alert in anticipation of the most glorious fifty seconds of his life.

Then suddenly they were off.

The masses packed in the stands screamed and shouted with excitement right from the moment the gun fired. Cec utilised his lightning acceleration to burst away from the tight melee at the start to claim the inside line before the first bend. His long, graceful stride required less contact with the energy sapping, time-consuming soft track. It was as if the crowd was an audience at a ballet, such was the beauty of his movement. Some held their breath in suspense, others cheered loudly as he kept the pack at bay to maintain a narrow lead as he bore down on the jostling group of six men waiting to start the second leg, each elbowing his neighbour to make room for an unhindered baton change. The second-leg athletes had to concentrate hard on when to start their run, hoping to gain a metre on the opposition without running out of the handover zone or dropping the baton. Cec put the baton into Lindsay's hand and stepped onto the infield, his job done. He watched the Blackheath Harrier, ten years his senior, accelerate away with the baton safely held in a vice-like grip. The noise level was already high, but as Lindsay emerged from the confusion and clashes of the first change in the lead, the decibel level increased to fever pitch.

It was an ideal first leg. 50.6 seconds passed Cec by in an adrenaline-fuelled blur. He had pulled a five-metre lead over his rivals, giving himself and Lindsay a crucial advantage in the scrum of the first baton change. It had been a gruelling effort and between gasps for air he looked towards Ainsworth-Davis and Butler, each a further ten metres down the straight because of the stagger, hoping for a sign of approval from them. Despite concentrating on Lindsay's progress and the preparations for their own legs, both returned his gaze and in unison gave him a respectful nod as if to say 'well done'.

Lindsay maintained the five-metre lead but Ainsworth-Davis let it slip to three metres on his leg. When Butler set off on the final lap of the track, Cec had recovered and cheered like he had never done before, adding to the cacophony of sound bouncing around the stadium. Rudd, the determined South African and individual 400 metres champion, started his anchor leg in fourth position but quickly closed the gap, overtaking his rivals to move up to third, then second. In the drag to the line, Butler was able to do enough to cross ahead of Rudd.

When Butler broke the cord, the euphoria in the stadium reached a peak and as he stood, chest heaving, still holding the baton, he was overwhelmed by official photographers who lined up the rest of the team beside him before he had recovered his composure. By chance, they assembled shoulder to shoulder in height order; 6 foot, 3 inch Guy Butler at one end and Cec, a head shorter, at the other.*

Rudd had stormed round the track in exactly 49 seconds, adding a silver medal to his gold in the 400 metres and bronze in the 800 metres. Butler (49.9) set the next fastest time in the race, nearly a second slower than Rudd. Cec (50.6) was third quickest; solid evidence that he probably missed out on an individual medal. Lindsay was fourth fastest (50.7), Ainsworth-Davis performed well enough (51.0) for the team to bring home the honours.

The value of Cec's early lead cannot be overvalued. The non-staggered start practically guaranteed, in a close race, that the first change would be frenetic – and so it proved to be. The American Schiller and Swede Krokstrom collided at the end of their first leg run as did France's distinguished fighter pilot André and South African Dafel. The five-metre lead that Butler held over Rudd when he crossed the line was the same five-metre lead that Cec had worked for.

---

* The image captured the effort and elation of their historic win but it lay forgotten in a private collection for many decades until unearthed by me in 2012.

Unsurprisingly *The Times* proudly reported the win, but their careful choice of words gave all the credit to Cambridge University AC runners Ainsworth-Davis and Butler. Praise was lavished on Ainsworth-Davis for passing a three-metre lead to Butler, when he actually began his leg with a bigger lead. As for Butler, he was painted the hero of the hour, bearing all responsibility for the team's victory. Cec was only mentioned as running the first quarter. At least the article graciously acknowledged them collectively, saying, 'The British team have maintained their optimism and determination throughout, and they fully deserve their successes.'

Just a few friends with a voice in the press and the Welsh newspapers credited Cec publicly as the architect of the relay success. Joe Binks, in the *News of the World* wrote, 'He practically won the mile [sic] by setting up a splendid first lap lead, which was never lost.' The *South Wales Echo* reported, 'He ran in dashing style, beating the Frenchman and the South African with the greatest ease and winning by six yards. This virtually won the relay race for England.' The same newspaper informed readers that a letter from Cecil's mother explained the cause of her son's indisposition for the individual 400 metres as being due to 'bad water', which affected Cec and two other athletes.

The 1920 Olympics was the last in which competitors received their medals at the closing ceremony. It is not known how many of the British athletes stayed to attend the presentation on 30 August, but Cec certainly did, as proved by his autograph book. Many of the signatures were of competitors from the last week of the Games, including British swimmers Lillian Birkenhead and Charlotte Radcliffe who competed on 29 August.

King Albert performed the ceremony in sunny conditions under a small covered stand in the stadium watched by nearly 30,000, the largest crowd of the Games. It must have been a slick operation; in just over an hour he presented in excess of 450 gold, silver and bronze medals together with several rows of small bronze statuettes awarded to every winner of an individual event. The brevity of the ceremony and the large number of awards suggests a rapid operation, a procession of athletes stepping up to receive their awards with a backdrop of seamless applause. The AAA arranged their engraving at a later date, so the athletes who did personally receive them from King Albert must have immediately surrendered them to Colonel Kentish.

Cec's magnificent gold medal, a true work of art, was designed by the Belgian sculptor José Dupon. It was made of sterling silver, weighing 79 grams, covered with thin gilt containing just six grams of gold, minted by Coosemans of Brussels. The 1912 Olympic Games had awarded pure gold medals, but the post-war economy precluded such an indulgence and economies had to be made.

On the obverse of the medal, a tall, naked athlete holds a palm leaf and laurel crown, symbols of victory, with the figure of Renommée or Truth playing the trumpet behind him. In the background there is a frieze with a Greek motif inscribed 'VII Olympiad'. The reverse celebrates the naming of Antwerp, depicting the statue in front of the town hall of Silvius Brabo, a Roman soldier, who in antiquity had slain the giant terrorising the river Scheldt. The mythical giant, Antigoon, had been demanding a toll from sailors using the river and cut off the hand of those who refused. Brabo had taken revenge and the statue shows him symbolically throwing the severed hand of the dead Antigoon into the river. Hence the name of the city, Antwerpen, which means 'thrown hand'. The port and the cathedral are shown in the background and the top of the medal is inscribed 'Anvers MCMXX'.

The medal was finely engraved along its edge with a considerable amount of information: '1600 Meters Relay * U.K * 1st * C. Griffiths & (G.M. Butler, J.C.A. Davis, R.A. Lindsay.)'

Only one Welsh track or field athlete had previously won an Olympic gold medal – David Jacobs in the 4x100 metres relay at the 1912 Games. Cec and Jack Ainsworth-Davis took the total to three.*

Cec was mildly upset not to receive the impressive cast bronze statuette awarded to the winners of individual events. Just 37 centimetres tall, it depicts a victorious athlete with his arm raised, holding a laurel wreath standing on a base inscribed 'Victoire' and signed by the artist, Léandre Grandmoulin. It was a very attractive prize and Cec would probably have considered Albert very fortunate to be carrying home two of these trophies to match the two marble busts he had won in Belgium before the war. As a consolation, Cec was presented with a bronze competitor's medal which

---

* Only one more has been won since that glorious day on 23 August 1920. Lynn Davies was victorious in the long jump at Tokyo in 1964 to become the only Welsh individual winner of an Olympic track and field gold medal and has reaped the rewards of fame ever since. Colin Jackson, despite being the world record holder for the 110 metres hurdles between 1993 and 2004, never quite achieved it, winning silver at 1988 in Seoul.

was equal in its elegance and size to the winner's medal, and a neat gold lapel pin of the newly introduced five ringed Olympic symbol.

Cec also had to fit the Olympic Diploma into his suitcase. Signed by the IOC President Baillet-Latour, 1,350 copies were printed, one for every athlete to stand on the podium. Designed by Pivat Livemont, it depicted the crowning of a naked Greek Olympian within a grand arena where a chariot race is in progress, the city of Antwerp is the backdrop. Only seven were taken home by victorious British athletes: two by Albert, one by Percy Hodge and one each for the relay team. Measuring 55x72 centimetres, it was too large to hang on the wall of his Stratford lodgings and was lucky to survive to the present day.*

Cec also acquired an Olympic flag. Rumour has it that he was the only one in the team agile enough to shin up the pole to unfasten it, but from exactly where it was taken is a secret long forgotten. There originally were about two hundred such flags made from Irish or Belgian linen, but apart from Cec's souvenir only one other is known to exist – the flag which was raised at the opening ceremony. It hung from a 15-foot flag pole in the Beerschot Stadium throughout the Games and was intended to be handed on from one Olympics to the next, but it was stolen before the closing ceremony. A replacement was provided for 1924 which lasted until 1988 at Seoul, when it was found to be too frayed and torn for further use. For 77 years, the whereabouts of the 1920

---

* In 1976 it was rescued from a lifetime of unprotected loft storage which had resulted in severe damage. It was crushed and torn nearly completely in half, but its restoration, combined with a suitably grand frame, have returned it to its former glory and it now proudly adorns our home.

flag remained a mystery until, in 1997, Hal Haig Prieste, the American bronze medallist platform diver, admitted pilfering it. He was 101 years old when his conscience caught up with him, explaining that he had taken it as a dare. He was worried that he wouldn't be around for much longer and handed it back to the IOC at the 2000 Olympics with an apology. He received the grateful thanks of the IOC – his action and careful storage of the precious flag had ensured its survival, enabling them to display it at their museum in Lausanne. He died in April 2001, his conscience clear.*

During the long days when Cec was not competing, he acquired several photographic postcards upon which he made notes about his experiences and filled a notebook with the signatures of athletes, gymnasts, swimmers and many others from the various sporting disciplines underway in the city. From that book we know Joe Binks was a spectator at the Games, probably at work for the *News of the World*, and he would have signed his name on those pages with pride.

Cec also rubbed shoulders with legends like Paavo Nurmi, the near-unbeatable long distance maestro who, like Cec, made his Olympic debut at Antwerp. On another of his postcards home, a star-struck Cec wrote, 'Missing you dreadfully but it is a privilege to be in the presence of a phenomenon such as Nurmi. Here is a man who will do great things.' Cec did not manage to obtain the autograph of the man who, slight in build but great in stature, returned

---

* Cec's flag also made it to the twenty-first century, preserved in the dark briefcase with his father's Navy insignia, so there remains two examples of the 1920 Olympic flag. Both items are identical in terms of design, material, hue and colouring but Prieste's is larger in keeping with its status as the official ceremony flag. Unlike Prieste, Cec never owned up and explained where his flag came from!

to Finland with three gold medals. Charley Paddock, the American sprint specialist, also won three medals – two gold and one silver. Six months younger than Cec, Paddock marginally failed to enter the record books as one of the few athletes to win an Olympic title as a junior when he won the 100 metres five days after his twentieth birthday.

The 1920 Olympics was a new dawn for British athletics after the long years of war. Some athletes like Albert Hill managed to belatedly squeeze onto the international stage, making up for missing out in 1916. However, the greater story was in the new generation of athletes that was beginning to make a mark. A.B. George in *All Sports Weekly* had some prophetic words regarding Cec and his fellow Olympic debutants:

> Of the younger runners we must look to in the future who ran at Antwerp, one must mention W.A. Hill, H.M. [Harold] Abrahams, C. Griffiths, J. Ainsworth-Davis, Guy Butler and E.W. [sic] Mountain.

He ended the article with great confidence about the continued success of the Olympics. The AAA could not disagree more. Their report of the 1920 Games pulled no punches, seriously criticising the IOC. They had issues with the poor organisation of the sports and accused the programme of being nothing more than an advertising medium which omitted too many names of competitors. This was a cardinal sin as far as the AAA was concerned, as their rules prevented athletes from competing if they were not included in the programme. As a result of their grievances, the AAA Special

Olympic Committee agreed a savage resolution for submission to the General Committee of the IOC:

> The International Olympic Committee is not composed of men with a sufficient general knowledge of sport and further, they have not taken proper steps to carry out regulations and decisions previously agreed upon, it is therefore thought necessary that the International Committee should be reorganised and composed of men who have a practical knowledge of Sport... The new body must have absolute control of the Games in the Country holding the Olympiad with full powers to enforce their rulings and regulation.

It would be interesting to know how it was received.

The AAA also censured the BOA over the financing and general arrangements for the British Olympic team. The AAA remained unconvinced whether future Olympic participation was worthwhile, and if it was decided to continue, they were determined that it would be on their own terms. The BOA was left near bankrupt, so much so that in 1922 they requested that the AAA assist them with current expenses. The response was a polite refusal.

The medals and statuettes acquired by the British team at Antwerp were forwarded, duly engraved, to the athletes who won them as it was deemed not practicable to have a public presentation. Of all the mean, unpatriotic and emotionless decisions made by the AAA in their Olympic history, this must rank as one of their worst. The usual Oxbridge cohort had failed to deliver and, of the six track and field gold medallists, three were from a working-class background. It seemed that this Olympic Games could not be over quick enough for the AAA.

Friends across the Channel – Gaston Féry and Cec

8

ENTENTE

CORDIALE

1920-1921

No fanfares, parades or press adulation welcomed the successful Olympians home, only ardent sports enthusiasts and *The Times* readers would have realised they had been competing in Belgium. Albert Hill's railway employers were gracious enough to organise a staff collection on his behalf, purchasing gifts for him and his wife with the money raised. Accepting cash would have been a blatant breach of the amateur code, but gifts were a circumnavigation of the rules that Harry Barclay and the AAA could do little about – athletes could receive prizes to the value of £7.7s., but not in cash. Ted Vowles welcomed Cec back to the shirt factory, but nothing more. Cec's work and athletic careers soon returned to normal.

On 4 September 1920, twelve days after his Olympic triumph, Cec made his debut in the Welsh Championship, the first holding of the event since 1914, at Newport Athletic Grounds. It was with great pride he travelled to the Gwent coastal town with May, who saw him come second in the 100 yards and win his first Welsh title in the 440 yards with a time of 51.4 seconds. This was only a tenth of a second outside David Jacobs' 1914 Welsh record, and a second outside the same athlete's best performance by a Welshman, set in 1910.

Welsh and British records took a different format in Cec's era compared to the present day – they recorded the best performances in Wales or Britain by athletes of any nationality. That left open the possibility that the Welsh record could be held by a non-Welsh runner, and the British record by a non-British runner. Moreover, if a Welsh athlete ran a quick time outside Wales – like David Jacobs did in the 440 yards at Herne Hill in 1910 – it did not count towards a Welsh record. The same occurred if a British athlete ran overseas.

There was no official recognition of the best performance by Welsh and British athletes (what we would now consider the modern Welsh and British records) although athletics historians have painstakingly researched to trace the best performances by Welsh and British athletes to Cec's era and beyond. However Cec's achievements were recorded, they proved his dominance in Welsh running for the next decade.*

On the same day as the Welsh Championship, athletes began to gather at the slightly grander Queen's Club in London for the British Empire Meeting between the returning USA Olympic team and a combined team of the British Empire. It was of particular significance as the inaugural event organised by Achilles Club.

In the face of a perceived threat to the status quo from athletes outside of the traditional university birthing grounds, Philip Noel-Baker and Bevil Rudd, past members of Cambridge University AC and Oxford University AC respectively, formulated the concept of a new club. It was formed in March 1920 with membership only open to past and present members of the Oxford and Cambridge athletics clubs. Achilles Club was unquestionably elitist. Its objectives were to nurture excellence and provide an organisation responsible for looking after the interests of its invariably privileged members. Noel-Baker was determined to raise the standard of British athletes for future Olympics and thought that the best way to do this was to promote athletics within the groups that he thought were most likely to succeed: Oxford and Cambridge students and alumni. The measure of Achilles' success is that it still exists today with the same

* In 1948 the creaking and archaic system of monitoring the best performances by athletes was altered. The old British record became known as the British all-comers' record. A new British national record noted the best performance in Britain by athletes born in Britain (or the Commonwealth). In the same year the Welsh AAA was formed which governed athletics throughout Wales and administered Welsh records on similar terms. It was not until 1960 that UK national records for performances made anywhere in world by British athletes were introduced.

conditions of membership and a history of national and international success which is unparalleled in Great Britain. At the time that it was formed, it was yet another old boys' network that Cec was not part of.

The following weekend, but still part of the same British Empire Meeting, the Victory Relays were held at Stamford Bridge. For Cec, the British Empire Meeting was less about the formation of a new athletics club than it was about another career-defining moment – his first British record. Cec ran in the 4x440 yards relay as part of a foursome representing the British Empire, although his colleagues were all Surrey AC teammates: Edgar Mountain, Dennis Bullough and Fred Mawby.

They crossed the line first and broke the twelve-year-old British record in a time of 3:20.8. Cec rounded the track in 49.8, knocking over half a second off his Olympic time despite it being over the slightly longer imperial distance; a magnificent performance. Mountain achieved the same time as Cec. Mawby (50.2) came close to breaking the 50-second barrier, while Bullough (51.0) made up for failing to gain a place in the relay team at Antwerp by writing his name in the history books. Having run the equal-fastest leg, Cec may have been presented with the team's bamboo baton. Certainly, Cec treasured one particular baton and kept it in his memorabilia.*

---

* This baton is still in the family and was originally thought to be the one used in the Olympic relay. However, a photograph discovered in 2012 of the 1920 Olympic relay team shortly after their victory (see p.80) shows Guy Butler holding a bamboo baton with a distinctive stem ring pattern different to the one in Cec's memorabilia. Butler likely did not relinquish his grip on the Olympic baton, so Cec probably seized the chance to keep the record-breaking baton instead.

Cec wrote many letters to his mother during this period, obviously missing his family and May. Few of those snapshot accounts of his life in London have withstood the ravages of time, but in one touching letter soon after the Victory Relay, he gives us a glimpse of the life of a young Welshman coping with a busy life in London, without much money and missing home.

Dear Ma and all,

Just a few lines to let you know that I am quite all right etc, but would much prefer to be home. We ran great in the Relay, Mountain did 49 4/5th, and I also did 49 4/5th, for our respective quarters, and the other two chaps ran extraordinarily well. Between us we broke the Mile Relay record, run in four quarters, the record has been standing for 12 years and Mr Vowles is very pleased with us. He is going to apply for the record to be recognised and I hope he gets it all right. I told Mr Vowles I wanted to go home Saturday night but he wanted me to stop. He suggested May should come up for a few days and I have written May asking if she'll come. He has found a place for her to stay and as it will not cost her anything, I think it will a nice little holiday for her, so don't stop her if she'll come.

I am writing this in Mr V's office. I stayed Saturday night with him and all day yesterday, but I felt very lonely and dumpy, and would much preferred to have been home.

I think Cyril Vowles, Billy Hill and I will go to see Tommy Phillips boxing at the ring tonight, I hope he will win. Mr Vowles has not given me any money yet, but I hope he will do so today.

Jim Hatton ran a great race in the three miles handicap on Saturday. The people cheered him and a few of the boys carried him. Mountain also ran well in the half mile handicap which he won. I did not compete in that event, but ran jolly well in the relay.

Well Chuggie! I think this is all for the present so will close now.
With lots of Love and Heaps of kisses.
Your Ever Loving Boy.
Cec XXXXXXXXXXXXXXXXXX

Ted Vowles, in whose office Cec wrote the letter, was one of the prime movers in his life. However, the enemies he had made in the quest to push his men to the top were beginning to circle. At a meeting of the AAA Southern Committee on 22 April 1921, a report was received from the Southern Counties Cross-Country Association. It levelled a series of serious allegations against Vowles regarding repeated breaches of AAA rules, mainly regarding athlete eligibility, dating back to 1919. It was even contemplated that 'certain members of the Surrey Athletic Club are ineligible for competition being employees of the Secretary of the Club'. They were serious charges, but it was decided that no action be taken against him. It had been a close call which nearly resulted not only in Ted being entered in the AAA's 'Black Book', but also his employee, Cec.

Also in April, the man who had so influenced Cec's destiny, William Trick, died at the age of 60.* William had been the nearest thing to a father for Cec and his intercession had helped Cec at two crucial moments in his life – finding him employment when he left school, and finding him a place in the Queen's Westminster Rifles. William also influenced

---

* His memory continues to live on in a commemorative stone laid in the wall at the entrance to Neath's indoor market in Green Street when it was built in 1904. The well-weathered but legible stone is still there and the market still thrives in the same building.

Cec's athletics career, encouraging Cec to run in the races that he sponsored during the war.

Life went on for Cec, who was now self-sufficient, employed in London and one of the country's top athletes. Even so, he could have done with some advice from his now-deceased uncle about feeling comfortable at society occasions. On 21 June, Surrey AC held their annual Ladies Night Dinner at the Clarendon Restaurant, Hammersmith. Sam Mussabini was one of the guests at the entertainment-packed evening, which saw Percy Hodge sing one of the songs. The guest list read like a who's who of British athletics so Cec passed around his menu for all to sign. He was somewhat awestruck by the occasion and perplexed by the sumptuous nine-course menu in French. He felt out of his depth until Jack Gillis, who realised that he needed a boost in confidence, came to his aid. He pointed out that of all the athletes in the room, only one other, Percy Hodge, had an Olympic gold medal in their pocket. Cec then relaxed to enjoy the dinner. When he shook Jack's hand at the end of the evening, a solid friendship had been formed.[*]

In the AAA Championship on 2 July, Cec was third for the third successive year in the 440 yards. Robert Lindsay beat Bevil Rudd by a foot in 50.4 seconds. Jack Ainsworth-Davis came fourth, meaning that four Olympic relay medal-

---

[*] Exactly the same situation arose at the 2012 Welsh Sports Hall of Fame dinner to celebrate Cec's induction, which I attended as his representative and custodian of his Olympic gold medal. I found myself seated beside Lynn Davies, 1964 Olympic gold medallist, and Rhodri Morgan, former First Minister of the Welsh Assembly. John Disley, 3,000 metres steeplechase bronze medallist at Helsinki in 1952, asked in what capacity I was attending the function. The most effective way to answer his question was to show him Cec's medal in my pocket and it was soon displayed alongside Lynn Davies' medal – a unique and historic occasion.

lists took the first four places. Indeed, each of the medallists won a heat in front of the 6,000 crowd on Friday evening in something of a tribute to their success at Antwerp.

Cec came within 2.2 seconds of his first AAA Championship win in the mile medley relay (four legs of 880, 220, 220 and 440 yards) for Surrey AC. Cec ran his favoured distance in the last leg, but he was beaten to the line by Polytechnic Harriers' Harry Edward, who was actually a sprint specialist. The Harriers must have had a strong team to place Edward, who had won the individual 100 and 220 yard races earlier in the meeting, on the longer last leg.

Many of the big names were missing from the third Triangular International Contest, held at Windsor Park in Belfast on 9 July 1921. It coincided with one of the most violent periods in the history of Northern Ireland. The troubles in the city had reached boiling point in the Irish War of Independence.

Rarely has an athletics meeting taken place in such an unstable location. The British Government's bounty of £10,000 on information leading to the capture of Michael Collins, the leader of the Irish resistance, was still on offer as Windsor Park filled with excited racegoers. Within the sound of the cheering crowd, the IRA ambushed an armoured truck of the Royal Irish Constabulary on Raglan Street, near the infamous Falls Road, killing one officer and injuring two more. A curfew was imposed over the weekend as the conditions for a truce were negotiated, but that did not prevent the deaths of sixteen civilians and 160 houses being destroyed.

It was hardly surprising that the best English athletes, including Cec, failed to compete. Scotland took advantage of English absenteeism and won the three-way challenge. The 440 yards was won by Scot G. Stevenson of Shettleston Harriers in a very modest 53 seconds, something that would surely have been beaten if Cec had been there. Prudence was the name of the game that day.

Eric Liddell played a major part in Scotland's victory, winning the 100 yards and 220 yards in close races with William Hill and Fred Mawby, Cec's friends from Surrey AC. Born in 1902 to missionary parents working in China for the Church of Scotland, Liddell only came to live in his home country when he entered Edinburgh University in 1920. His appearance in Belfast for the Triangular International was his debut in athletics outside of Scotland. He probably considered the strife in Ireland to be minor compared with the suffering and breach of human rights he had witnessed in China's regular civil wars.

Although he missed out on the chance of a victory in Belfast, the rest seems to have done Cec good. At the Welsh Championship held at Barry Island Athletic Club on 16 July 1921, run round a tight, bumpy 330-yard grass track, Cec won two titles and entered the record books for both. In the 220 yards his 23.0 equalled J. Gorman's 1908 Welsh record; in the 440 yards his 49.8 broke David Jacobs' 1914 Welsh record and also became the best ever performance by a Welshman, beating Jacobs' 1910 time. His 49.8 stood as the best performance in Wales for 30 years and the best performance by a Welshman for 32 years. For the metric 400 metres it converted to 49.5, which would have been good enough to win the 2012 Welsh title.

The furore over the capability of sending teams to compete in international competition that nearly ended British participation in the 1920 Olympics seemed to have died down the following year. On 11 September 1921, the first athletics contest between England and a continental country was held at the Stade Colombes in Paris. The British team stayed in the Hotel Lutetia and on the morning of the event Cec sent a postcard of the ostentatious hotel to May in Neath. He admitted to being nervous about the afternoon but promised to do his best and would write her a long letter when he returned to London as he was missing her very much.

The Fraternité Cup attracted the largest crowd to an athletics meeting in France, but it was not necessarily a popular event. The idea behind it was to strengthen the post-war alliance, but the timing was unfortunate. The French people were angry following the British Treasury's action over exchange rates which had devalued the franc. Many who gained entry by storming the barriers invaded the track, but the worst act of protest displayed that Saturday was the stoning of the bus carrying the British team when it arrived at the stadium. If Cec had been nervous earlier in the day when he wrote the postcard, one can only imagine his concern about facing the crowd as abuse and missiles were hurled at the team's transport. The visiting athletes were further angered because the French had changed the scoring system for the meeting without consultation.

Cec was entered for the 400 metres and one of his opponents was Gaston Féry, who had been a member of the bronze winning French relay team at Antwerp the year before. There was no separating them in the race and they breasted the tape side by side. Féry was declared the winner but the usually partisan crowd thought the Englishman had won by a few inches, so gave a whistling demonstration of disapproval against the decision. Their political protests which threatened the entente cordiale had not affected their sense of fair play and justice on the race track, especially when it involved such a mild-mannered athlete.

Later in the day, Cec had revenge in the medley relay, a popular race for competitors and spectators. The English team, each having won their individual events, were all Surrey AC members; Edgar Mountain on the crucial opening 800 metre leg; Lancelot Royle (who became Sir Lancelot in 1948) and William Hill sprinting over 200 metres and Cec competing directly against Féry on the last leg in a re-run of their 400 metres clash earlier in the afternoon. Medley relays are often decided on the first leg – a long lead at the halfway stage is not easily made up by the other three. That was not the case on this occasion – the baton was handed over to the last runners at almost exactly the same time. Cec and Gaston battled for the lead all around the last lap, but victory by Cec for the English team ensured the Fraternité Cup was narrowly won by the visitors. He and Gaston enthusiastically congratulated each other, exchanging handshakes and running vests; it was another close friendship that Cec formed with a fellow athlete. They posed together with arms linked for a photograph which was rapidly processed, upon which Gaston wrote a warm tribute to their memorable contest, 'à l'ami Griffiths. Un souvenir d'une belle lutte sportive. G. Féry France angleterre 11.9.21.' Cec treasured the French running shirt, photograph and medals from his first visit to France for the rest of his life.*

The two small lozenge-shaped medals Cec won were undeniably French, featuring a strutting cockerel. They were inlaid with delicate enamelled flags of France and Great Britain and engraved with the date, 11 September 1921. Unusually, considering the era and the importance of the contest, they did not contain any precious metal, perhaps because it was the inaugural staging of the Fraternité Cup.

The careers of Cec, his relay partners in France and Henry Stallard, who won the 1,500 metres at the Stade Colombes, would be closely entwined for most of the decade. Stallard was a year younger than Cec and both would shift from the event in which they first made their name to compete against each other for the title of the best British half miler a few years later.

On a Thursday evening on 15 September, Cec won a 660 yards handicap off scratch at Paddington with 1:21.4, which was 2.4 seconds inside Hector Phillips' British record set at Stamford Bridge in 1916. For some reason it did not satisfy the necessary criteria to be ratified, be it an issue with the track, timing or insufficient grade of officials present.

Cec would break many records over his career, but he would face more than his fair share of difficulties. Even if a runner managed to beat one of the records and it was deemed to fit the criteria, the athlete may not have been

---

* One of the many touching aspects of my research was the bringing together of the postcard written to May before the Fraternité Cup with his endorsed photograph from Gaston taken afterwards. Only a few hours had passed between the two items being written, but that short time captured so many emotions as the two great men made sporting history.

credited with it. The officials had to be certain that the conditions for breaking a record had been met – an athlete may be denied the record if the track was not sanctioned, or the officials and timekeepers were not sanctioned, and in an era where timekeeping was not an exact science, the runner had to win the race – the other places were not officially timed. It was a maze filled with potential hazards that meant many athletes, including Cec, were denied records for perfectly sound performances.

A.B. George summarised the 1921 season in his column in *All Sports Weekly*. He raised a controversial point regarding British athletes generally, but he was specific in his comments about two members of the newly-formed Achilles Club:

> It is rather disappointing that we have many fine athletes, such as G.M. Butler and J. Ainsworth-Davis, to name two, who fail to attain the fame one anticipates because they apparently lack time or enthusiasm to get the best out of themselves.

George's criticism could not have been more incisive regarding Ainsworth-Davis. As yet unbeknown to him, Ainsworth-Davis had actually terminated his involvement in athletics at the end of the season when he left Christ's College Cambridge to study medicine at St Bartholomew's Hospital in London. His two-year career must be one of the shortest on record for the winner of an Olympic gold medal. He was clearly a man driven; he had served with distinction and honour during the war, progressing from the Army to the Royal Flying Corps, he supported his family through his medical studies by playing in a band, and upon qualifying as a doctor and retiring from athletics became a highly qualified and accomplished urological surgeon.

Yet Ainsworth-Davis' temporary involvement in athletics was not unusual for an elite university athlete. Their short running careers were an indication of the priority they attached to it in relation to their long-term ambitions. Many considered athletics to be something that occupied their time while they were studying to forge a career and, like Ainsworth-Davis, abandoned the tracks once they qualified as doctors, lawyers or whatever profession they entered. This attitude would persist for several decades.

THE ATHLETIC INTERNATIONAL.

Who needs photographers?
The *Daily Express* report on
the Fraternité Cup, and Cec's
meeting with King George V
at the AAA Championship.

9

A WEDDING FIT
FOR A KING
1922

Cec suffered a leg injury during 1921 which he ascribed to the demands of the 440 yards. Guy Butler, tall and muscular, was the epitome of an athlete who was more robust and suited for the long sprint distance. Cec's compact physique suited middle-distance running, where his combination of speed and stamina would be most effective. It could be argued – Olympic gold medal aside – that he wasted his formative years by choosing the wrong event.

Proof would soon be forthcoming in a couple of experimental 880 yards (half mile) races at the end of 1921 which did not go unnoticed by observers in the press, including the outspoken A.B. George:

> When this stylish mover won a fast half mile at High Wycombe, the experts became alive to the fact that he was probably better at four furlongs than the "quarter"... If Griffiths trains specially for the "half" next season, he is quite likely to show us 1min 56 secs under favourable conditions.

Despite his Olympic medal, Cec had only come third at the 440 yards at the AAA Championships three years in succession. Joe Binks suggested he moved up to 880 yards which he felt better suited his style and allowed him to adopt a more tactical approach to take advantage of his electric finishing sprint, rather than running flat out from the gun.

Over the mild winter Cec considered a change to the longer distance. He had some big running shoes to fill, notably those of Albert Hill who had recently retired, but that also left the field clear for a new entrant. It was not a difficult decision for him to make. It came as no surprise to the athletics fraternity when Cec decided to concentrate on the half mile and he explained his decision to change events in the *South Wales Echo*:

> There was a time when I thought myself a quarter miler, but I felt that I could not stand the strain, and when my leg broke down I decided to concentrate on the half mile. I cannot say I am sorry, because the 440 yards is a really gruelling race,

and one mistake means losing it, whereas the half mile gives one more time to think, and a chance to make up for any lost distance. Just as a jockey works his horse into a favourable position on the course, so an athlete must use his head to his own advantage if he is to be a successful distance runner.

Cec was clearly enthusiastic about the new season and attended the annual general meeting of the AAA on behalf of Surrey AC at the Royal Society of Arts in London on 8 April 1922.[*] Once the season started, he continued to familiarise himself with the longer runs. His first major victories in the newly-adopted distance came in two meetings over two days on 9 and 10 June. On Friday he won the first of three titles in the annual championship meeting of the AAA Southern Committee with a respectable 2:02.0. The next day at Stamford Bridge in the Kinnaird Trophy, a contest organised by Achilles against several clubs from the south of England, he beat Douglas Lowe in a much quicker 1:58.0. This was the best known performance by a Welshman at that distance. This debut win in the 880 yards heralded seven consecutive years of success at Kinnaird Trophy meetings, where he was always in the top three.

A week later on 17 June Cec was back at Chelsea's Stamford Bridge for the Civil Service Sports meeting. On this occasion, he entered the only mile race that he is known to have taken part in, coming sixth in a time of 4:25.4. Although his position was relatively lowly, it was a time that beat the Welsh record – although Cec was given a 35 yard

[*] In the AAA archives at Birmingham University, I found the list signed by those attending the AGM and with great excitement saw Cec's name written in his distinctive, neat handwriting below those of Jim Hatton and Cyril Vowles, who were all representing Surrey AC.

head start. That probably saved him about six seconds and he beat the record by 4.6 seconds, but even so, it was a superlative first (and only) attempt at the mile, especially considering that the top two finishers both had more than an extra 100 yards start over him – the winner was P.A. Selman (Civil Service) in 4:20.0 from a 137 yard start, from H. Crudgington (Oxford House AC) off 143 yards and C.J. Webber (Luton H) off 57 yards.

Cec still entered 440 yards races, but he was enormously encouraged by his immediate competitiveness in his first half miles. He knew there was a lot more to come – not only championship success, but also new records. The most attractive one for him to contemplate was the 880 yards British record held by Mel Sheppard with 1:54.0. Sheppard, an American, had set the time in the 1908 London Olympics – he passed 800 metres in a world record 1:52.8 and, in anticipation of a quick time, officials had placed another tape at 880 yards, 4.7 metres further on. It was also a world record performance, subsequently broken by Ted Meredith in the 1912 Olympics, but the British record remained. The best performance by a British athlete, 1:54.6, was jointly held by Francis Cross (in Oxford) and Herbert Workman (in Montreal). Considering that Cec had already run within four seconds, the future looked promising.

The summer of 1922 would be one of the busiest and most demanding of his life, but it was also the most rewarding. The first day of July saw the AAA Championship at Stamford Bridge. Cec competed in his first half mile for the national title, a wet and windy thriller in front of 25,000 excited spectators, including King George V. The atmosphere was intoxicating; the buzz Cec experienced was the same as in the Olympic stadium at Antwerp. He welcomed the familiarity of it, hoping once again it would provide him with a winning edge against competitors who might be overawed by the occasion.

The crowd was unusually large for such a miserable and uncomfortable day, but there was a particular attraction which had drawn them. As usual, the AAA had invited overseas athletes to liven up proceedings and Paavo Nurmi, Cec's hero and treble gold medallist from the 1920 Olympics, was topping the bill. Cec was ecstatic to meet him again, cheering him on in the four miles race and two miles steeplechase, both of which he won easily in masterful style.

Not everybody welcomed the inclusion of foreign athletes competing at the AAA Championship. This was light-heartedly illustrated in the press with a report of a conversation between two friends. One asked who had won the mile. On being told that the honours had gone to the Scottish athlete, Duncan McPhee, he grunted, 'humph, another foreigner.' Perhaps Percy Hodge was warranted in being a little grumpy about foreign participation – in the two miles steeplechase, Nurmi's win prevented Hodge from taking his fourth successive AAA Championship title.

The soft, wet track and the strong summer winds were not conducive to fast times. Cec would have only concentrated on his finishing position, thinking that the time was irrelevant. He lined up alongside the defending AAA Champion, Edgar Mountain. Both had won their heats and a grand battle was anticipated.

In front of a roaring crowd, Cec led coming down the back straight on the second and final lap, but Mountain narrowly beat him on the line in a sprint finish. It was a thrilling duel. Perhaps Cec did not yet have the required stamina to beat the champion over the long distance. Perhaps he had not yet learned the perfect time to begin his sprint finish and went slightly too early or too late. Whatever the case, from the photograph taken of the finish it was impossible to see whether he, with number 13 pinned over his chest, or Mountain with 1 on his stomach, had won. They were both compact athletes and looked like twins as they broke the tape, identical in posture with chests dipped and arms spread behind them. Mountain narrowly took the win with 1:55.6 but Cec's time of 1:55.8 was the fastest ever for a Welsh athlete. Although only the winner was officially timed, the times for second and third places were estimates based on the distance behind the winner and usually quite accurate. However on this occasion the near dead heat suggests that Cec may have been over-penalised just a tad.* A.B. George's prediction that Cec would soon break 1:56.0 if he stepped up to the longer distance had been proved entirely accurate.

Cec did not leave the AAA Championship without a title – he set up the Surrey AC team to win the mile medley relay, this time running the first leg of 880 yards as opposed to the last leg of 440 yards which he ran the previous year. It would have been a happy occasion for close friends Cec, Lancelot Royle, William Hill and Jack Gillis.

---

* Cec would lower his time and retain the best performance by a Welsh athlete in the 880 yards for 37 years to confirm his status as the best Welsh middle-distance runner until 1959, when Tony Harris arrived upon the scene.

Cec was among the competitors who were introduced to the king, who talked with knowledge and interest about their achievements. The monarch was the same height as him, just over five and a half feet tall. He had been watching from near the finish line so had a commanding view of the tense climax to Cec's race, and sympathised with him on being beaten by a few inches.

Sport Pictures published a photograph of Cec with the king under the headline 'Greatest Athletes of the Year'. The only other 'great' to share the same pictorial tribute was Paavo Nurmi – an honour indeed considering that there were several AAA Champions such as Mountain or McPhee who they could have featured. Cec bought many copies of the publication for his family. The king must have been grateful for not being photographed with taller athletes who may have made him appear slightly less majestic.

At the end of the day, Percy Hodge walked out of the stadium accompanied by Harry Barclay and Lord Desborough. Hodge, head down and dejected, was not concentrating when somebody alongside him remarked, 'So you are the Olympic champion, I understand?'

'Yes, sir,' the dispirited Hodge replied, eyes still fixed on the wet pavement, 'but my stomach is all wrong today and I'm out of it.'

There was an uneasy silence. Hodge looked up and froze as he realised he was addressing His Majesty the King, who offered his hand to the embarrassed athlete. As he shook it, Hodge stammered out, 'Your Majesty, but I hope for better luck next time.' Shaken by his royal encounter he walked away feeling elated but awkward. He appreciated the king's words, later commenting, 'What a fine man His Majesty really is.'

Cec added more signatures to his collection at the championship dinner held that evening at the Monico Restaurant, Piccadilly Circus. Amongst the list of names which Cec accumulated on his menu there was one which was notably missing from his 1920 Olympic autograph book: Paavo Nurmi, the guest of honour, pencilled his name below Jack Gillis and Edgar Mountain. Cec would have been thrilled.

The foul summer weather remained a week later, on 8 July, for the Triangular International Contest in Glasgow. Cec won the 440 yards – he was still among the best at the shorter distance – and came second again in the 880 yards to Mountain. The Surrey pair romped ahead around the last bend to overtake the leading Scot, James Ponsford, and Mountain surged ahead. When he realised that an English one-two was certain, he held back and broke the tape linked arm in arm with Cec in a time of 2:01.0. It was a grand gesture by Mountain, who was still awarded the victory, and indicative of the friendship between the two best 880 yards runners in the country. Mountain was still the master, unbeatable; Cec was the student learning from his every move.

This was the first event at which Cec met Eric Liddell, the man who had helped guide Scotland to victory the year before. Known as the Flying Scotsman on account of his speed in the sprint events, Liddell was a true all-round sportsman. By the time he crossed paths with Cec, Liddell had already won three caps playing rugby on the wing for Scotland against France, Wales and Ireland, scoring the winning try against the Irish. If circumstances had been different for Cec, he may have joined D.D. Hiddlestone of Neath RFC to meet Liddell on the rugby field in Edinburgh on 4 February 1922 when Scotland and Wales drew 9-9. Liddell played in a further four matches during 1923 but failed to score any more tries.

After two years of residence in Stratford, which was a Parliamentary constituency in the Borough of West Ham in South West Essex, AAA rules allowed Cec to race for Essex. To this end he joined Southend Harriers. They had a particularly enterprising Secretary, George Hogsflesh, who probably was instrumental in signing up Cec as a member.

Cec will always be remembered as a Surrey AC man (which, despite its name, was not actually a county club), competing throughout his career in their white, black and blue strip at major events or in matches between other athletic clubs. However, he maintained his Southend Harriers membership for the Essex County Cycling and Athletic Association Championships (known more simply as the Essex Championships) and inter-county meetings where he met with great success in relays representing Essex.

Cec could have chosen to represent Glamorgan, the county of his birth, and there was some pressure from those quarters for him to do so. However, Essex offered a number of benefits. Not only was it the county in which he lived and therefore practical, but the President of the ECCAA, General Wigan, was a supporter of the Territorials and Cec's old regiment the Queen's Westminster Rifles. The most likely factor though was that three of his Surrey teammates and friends, Jack Gillis, William Hill and Jim Hatton, were already members of Southend Harriers. Together they probably had plans for an assault on the Inter-County Championship relays as an Essex team.

On 15 July, Cec entered the Essex county record books for the first time in their 37th annual championship held at the Castle Park cricket ground in Colchester. He won the half mile race 'magnificently' according to the *Chelmsford Chronicle*, but the soft rain-affected track meant a slow time of 2:07.2. His fellow Surrey and Southend friends were all successful; Hill won two 100 yards races, Hatton won the mile and three miles races (and with it the Atlanta Cup), Gillis won the 440 yards, all to retain their titles. Cec joined up with Gillis and Hill and L.H. Phillips to win the medley relay for Southend Harriers. The Surrey men were a formidable force but when representing Southend Harriers in a relay they always made sure to include a more established member of the club to avoid overt criticism of being a team of Surrey ringers.

In open relay races where club membership was not an issue, especially events which attracted the crowds and offered the best prizes, Cec, Gillis and Hill included one of Royle, Mountain or Hatton to make it an unashamed all-Surrey affair. The mile medley relay was a real crowd puller and promoters offered attractive prizes up to the AAA limit of £7.7s. to entice the best competitors. This relay was perfectly suited to teams with runners possessing a range of skills. With Cec setting up a lead on the long first leg and Gillis and Hill sprinting away to leave the last leg a virtual stroll for Royle, Mountain or Hatton, it was a sure recipe for success for the Surrey friends and they earned the moniker of The Untouchables. When Cec won the Aldershot Command open mile relay with them on 22 July, the white metal medal he won was his last as a single man.

On 25 July, Cec and May were married at St David's Parish Church in Neath, the same building where he had been christened and confirmed. Cyril Vowles was his best man and many of his friends travelled down to Wales to attend the midweek wedding which had to be slotted into his busy racing schedule. If he wasn't racing he was working. Visits home were rare, so buying an 18 carat Welsh gold wedding ring mattered to Cec. It had to be tiny to fit May's delicate finger.*

There was no chance of a honeymoon. On the 29 July he competed in the second England v France Fraternité Cup contest. Stamford Bridge was the venue of England's first ever home athletics international, and the novelty of the occasion attracted a crowd of 12,000. The political troubles of the previous year had been forgotten to make the return match a more pleasant occasion. The only signs of disapproval were from the home crowd in response to William Nichol being dubiously placed third in the 100 metres behind André and René Mourlon. Their objection concerned the celerity of the French brothers on the mark. This continental way of 'getting a run on the pistol' was spreading across the Channel, to the chagrin of the British competitors and spectators, causing the AAA to announce they would be looking into the whole subject of starting.

Cec was eager to meet Gaston Féry again, both as a friend and adversary. Cec won the 400 metres with Féry third. The

* Vanessa, having inherited her grandmother's thin wrists and fingers, is still able to wear this priceless family heirloom.

score with his French *ami* had been emphatically evened, but not with Mountain in the 800 metres. In another legendary duel, Mountain won the race, Cec came second again, with Douglas Lowe third and Féry fifth. The *Illustrated Sporting and Dramatic News* coverage of the meeting, won convincingly by England, stoked the Mountain-Griffiths debate: 'Which of these two club fellows and personal friends is really the better of the two at the half mile remains unsettled.'

In truth, results showed that Mountain was still the stronger, but Cec was a determined rival. The emergence of Lowe, Mountain's Cambridge University AC colleague, created another serious challenger for Cec.

The *Daily Express* cartoonist produced a pictorial of the Fraternité Cup featuring two images of Cec. On one, underneath a sketch of him at full stride, the caption reads 'C.R. Griffiths only got married last Tuesday but won the 400 metres on Saturday'. The other shows Mountain, Griffiths and Lowe finishing the 800 metres in close formation under a red rose flag of England with the explanation they 'put the kibosh on France'.

It was not often that Cec made a concerted effort to break a specific record. Not only were records often unratified by officials who were unhappy with a particular aspect of a performance or how it was measured, athletes also had far less interest in records and personal bests prior to the Second World War. However, at the start of August, Cec did make an exception at Stamford Bridge for one record which he had set his eyes on.

Sight was a precious commodity among the patients at St Dunstan's Hostel in Regent's Park, London. The hostel for blind people had been established in 1915, primarily for the care of casualties from the war, and provided a home for 150 residents. Many thousands also received medical care, rehabilitation and training to ease them back into as normal a life as possible. Sport was greatly encouraged. The lake in the park was used for swimming and rowing competitions, tug of war was popular, as were goal shooting contests against professional goalkeepers from clubs like Arsenal. It was all part of a treatment regime to restore physical ability and confidence in an entertaining manner, somewhat avant-garde for post-war Europe.

The annual athletics and cycling meeting at Stamford Bridge to raise funds for the hostel was the highlight in its calendar. There was a variety of races for the blinded heroes of the hostel using strings to connect them with able-bodied runners. The open races attracted top athletes who often attempted to break records under stage-managed but permissible conditions.

The 1922 St Dunstan's meeting on the evening of Monday 7 August was no exception. 12,000 spectators turned out to watch Cec's assault on Hector Phillips' 660 yards British record of 1:23.8 set on the same track in 1916. Cec had smashed this time the previous year at Paddington with 1:21.4, but for reasons unknown it was not ratified. He was certainly intending to take the record this time.

On a slow track due to overnight rain, Cec ran in a specially-framed limited handicap with the inside lane reserved just for him. The only runner starting on scratch, he had to overtake every competitor. One nearly spoiled the show – only by running the final straight at great pace did Cec win the race. However, the opponent was right to push Cec to the limit. With a time of 1:21.6, he shaved 2.2 seconds off the old record.

The photograph of Cec breaking the tape, wearing 1 on his Surrey AC, vest was on the front page of the *Daily Mirror* the next day. Arthur Pearson, the co-founder of the *Mirror's* publishing company, must have been pleased with the publicity – he was responsible for first funding St Dunstan's Hostel. The meeting was covered by several other national newspapers, including the *Daily Telegraph*, the *Daily Express* and the Welsh press who all extolled Cec's achievement in breaking the record, his second British record after the 4x440 yards relay in 1920. However, the claim for the record failed, probably for similar reasons to those which prevented his slightly faster race at Paddington the year before from being recognised too.

Cec did not have time to sit at home and read of his exploits in the newspapers. Two evenings later, on 9 August, he was in Scotland for a meeting held by Hibernian at Easter Road. This was a joint athletics and five-a-side football tournament enjoyed by a crowd of 10,000 and it attracted some big names in both sports. In the 600 yards invitation race (an unusual distance), Cec on scratch was narrowly beaten by G. Stevenson, the half mile winner in Belfast the previous year, who enjoyed a ten yards head start. The handicappers did an extraordinary job. All of the races were won by narrow margins, despite some athletes being given very generous handicaps. In the 880 yards, Mountain lost by one yard to a runner given 65 yards. In the 120 yards race, the local hope, Eric Liddell, was beaten by three-time AAA Champion Harry Edward. Despite being given a one yard start, Liddell lost by two.

Cec probably stayed in Scotland for the Celtic Football Club Sports the following weekend, his third meeting that week. The heavy rain kept the crowds away and only half of the expected 25,000 turned up to watch Liddell win the 120 and 220 yards invitation races. Cec was unexpectedly unplaced in the half mile, perhaps due to too much racing since the start of July, but the *Daily Record* still featured a cartoon of him, noting that 'this clean cut little Welshman has a taking style'.

Cec had a week to recover before the Welsh Championship on 19 August at Cardiff Arms Park, the home of Welsh sport. He took home two championship titles, in the 440 and 880 yards. His 880 yards time of 1:59.2, despite being nearly four seconds slower than his best time set a month earlier at Stamford Bridge, was the fastest ever in Wales and secured him the Welsh record, previously set in 1906, by 0.2 seconds.

A week later at the Metropolitan Police Sports held at the Herne Hill track in London, Cec and Mountain were the only two entered on scratch in the 880 yards handicap. It was their fourth meeting in recent weeks, but finally the student had something to teach the master. On the loose track, Cec won by ten yards in a personal best time of 1:55.2. It was only 1.2 seconds from Mel Sheppard's British record and beat his personal best time of 1:55.8 set at the AAA Championship eight weeks earlier, the best ever performance by a Welsh athlete. Cec got to take a gold watch home and helped Surrey AC to victory in the two miles relay, a race which comprised four 880 yards legs. By the halfway mark, F.W. Manton and R. Mitchell each had lost three yards to their South London Harrier opponents, but Cec regained the lead and handed it over to a safe pair of hands in Mountain, who went on to win the event in 8:35.8.

With Cec finally gaining a victory over Mountain, there were many more column inches devoted to who was the best half miler. They agreed to pose together for a photograph which ignited demands for a direct contest between them. Their races thrilled many thousands of paying spectators and pontificating experts; every one of them had their own opinion as to who was superior. Bare statistics arguably suggest that Cec achieved more over his career, but it was more diverse and longer than Mountain's. Many an observer would have disagreed on any given day.

As Surrey AC teammates, both Cec and Mountain brought a great deal of glory to the club. However, some of their opponents did not like the way that Surrey seemed to be able to cherry-pick the best talent. The Surrey system came under threat after a mile medley relay race at High Wycombe on 2 September 1922. Cec ran the first leg and set up his Surrey team for another win, but a protest was lodged against one of his teammates, R.N. Cracknell. The complainant alleged that Cracknell was a first-claim member of Wycombe Phoenix Harriers and had been a member of Surrey AC for less than three months. Once again, Ted Vowles had made a direct approach and seemed to be poaching a runner. The AAA Southern Committee launched an investigation and examined the Surrey AC subscription books, finding them unsatisfactory. Ted Vowles was questioned about the specific date on which Cracknell signed the Surrey application form. Vowles' explanation that the original application had been lost was not accepted so the protest was upheld. The meeting recorded, 'We regret that in his written statement, Mr Vowles was not entirely up front with the AAA.'

Ted Vowles' house of cards was about to come tumbling down. On 27 October, the Southern Committee voted to suspend him indefinitely from athletics or the management of athletics. He was not allowed to act as a starter or official at any race meeting, and certainly not able to become involved with any disputes his members had with the AAA. Cec would have been aware of the crisis within his club, but thought that it would not unduly affect him. He was wrong.

It was customary for athletes to rest over winter, but fuelled by his friendly rivalry with Mountain and keen to step up another level, Cec followed advice given to him by Albert Hill and kept a strict training schedule. He entered cross-country events to keep in condition, raising a few eyebrows in the athletics world. After all, trying too hard was a crime in their eyes.

Many athletes from the top echelon, including Cambridge University's Harold Abrahams and Oxford University's Roger Bannister, have held secret time trials to establish just how fast they could run. However, they hid their efforts from the media to avoid being criticised for trying too hard for an amateur. They were concerned that training or specialisation would expose them to the stigma of professionalism – they wanted to be cheered, not jeered. Had other athletes like Cec wanted to hire a track, timekeepers and officials, the cost would have been prohibitive.

Cec's cross-country races did not go against amateur regulations, they were just unusual. He came third in the 1922 South of Thames Cross-Country Championship on Epsom racecourse to Corporal W.M. 'Joe' Cotterell, the tough Birchfield Harrier, helping Surrey AC to take the team prize. In an interview, Cec explained:

> I enjoyed it thoroughly because I decided to jog along at my own pace and not worry about getting to the front. Most of us never saw Cotterell after the first mile or so. One has to be wonderfully fit for this kind of racing, however, and it is perhaps the best kind of training for track athletes, as it relieves the monotony of the enclosed space.

It's alright, he seemed to be saying. I wasn't really trying!

A narrow win for Mountain at the 1922 AAA
Championship (above). Sweet revenge (below).

10

FAMILY

MATTERS

1923

On 13 January 1923, Cec and May had a son, naming him John after Cec's great friend, John 'Jack' Gillis. In July, Gillis would earn a small place in racing history when Eric Liddell tripped over his legs in the 440 yards at the Triangular International Contest. Liddell fell heavily and lost 30 yards to the rest of the field, which he magnificently clawed back to beat Gillis at the tape. This race was regarded by most who witnessed it as the ultimate athletics display; victory snatched from the jaws of defeat. It was an echo of the race in 1915 at the Neath Great September Fair when Cec had been tripped, although in Liddell's case the clash was accidental and the fight back successful.

A photograph of May and John soon after he was born shows a radiant happy mother with a healthy baby, a welcome addition to her life with Cec being away so much during the athletics season. Finances dictated it impossible for her to accompany him to many races, so the company she had at home was a blessing.

The AAA Championship at Stamford Bridge dawned bright and temperatures soared as the sun climbed. A crowd of 16,000 poured into the stadium anticipating a good day's entertainment. A triumvirate of *Athletic News* correspondents; Outpost, Ubiquitous and Tityrus (the pseudonym of J.A.H. Catton, editor of the paper and the best football journalist in the country) reported on proceedings, each writing with an individual style but with a fair degree of duplication.

Outpost had high hopes for Cec in the 880 yards based on the Friday evening heats, when Cec won his race with plenty in reserve. Edgar Mountain, although also winning, looked lacklustre and was described as 'listless'.

Cec arrived on Saturday morning, confident in his abilities. He donned number 28 – perhaps happy that he had avoided unlucky 13, the number he wore in the previous year's close finish. Mountain was still the defending champion and number 1, but must have realised he faced a tough task to win a third consecutive title. Cec was improving all the time and the leading challenger for his crown.

As the six runners in the final lined up for the start, Tity-rus noted 'the quiet look of confidence on Griffiths' face'. The sun's strong rays disappeared and a slight breeze blew across the track. The air was still hot and there was an atmosphere of intense expectation as the spectators, officials and competitors readied themselves for the start.

From the gun, Douglas Lowe set a fast pace with Sydney 'Sonny' Spencer and Mountain in close pursuit. Cec hung a little further back. He waited, poised, until the second lap with 300 yards to go. Then Cec, keeping to the inside, moved up to third. With 200 yards remaining, Mountain made his move but Cec shadowed him for 50 yards before overtaking him and sprinting to the finish with the reigning champion endeavouring to hold on right to the line. Cec had done it – he had won his first individual AAA Championship title. Spencer was third, ahead of Lowe.

Cec had taken on board the change from 440 yards to 880 yards suggested by Joe Binks the previous year and in doing so, not only became an AAA British Champion but became the first AAA Champion on the track who had won an Olympic gold medal before winning his domestic championship. Only the Southern Irishman, Tim Ahearne, prevented that accolade being extended to cover field athletes – he had won the triple jump at the 1908 Olympic Games and the long jump at the 1909 AAA Championship.

The photograph of the finish was nearly identical to the 1922 race, except on this occasion Cec was the victor with a small margin of three yards in a time of 1:56.6. It was sweet revenge for his narrow defeat by Mountain on that occasion. Cec had beaten some fine runners to establish himself as leader of the very talented half mile pack and the gold medal he won completed his set, adding to the individual bronzes he won 1919, 1920 and 1921 and the silver in 1922.

Seventy minutes after his fabulous win, Cec turned out for the final of the 440 yards. Not surprisingly, his previous exertions in the high temperatures had exhausted him and, unusually, he did not finish. Cec went away strongly but quickly fell away from the leading pack, eventually leaving American invitee William Stevenson, Guy Butler and Jack Gillis to take the medals. In a particularly poetic account, *Athletic News* recorded:

> The Quarter Mile produced a struggle worthy of so great an event. Physically two competitors stood out by themselves – fine types of manhood. They were G.M. Butler of Cambridge University, and W. E. Stevenson, of Oxford University. On the mark they looked big enough to eat all their foes. No doubt in some fairy story of the Princess Beautiful either of them would have done so. But this was to be a real race among mortals. Butler was very anxious to get away quickly, and so was Griffiths, of the Surrey Athletic Club. When the starter dispatched them Butler, on the outside, went away at such a pace that he was leading the field in about 80 yards. I was astonished and wondered how soon he would give up the ghost. My neighbour said that he would either crack or smash record. He did neither, but as the bend for home was being traversed Stevenson joined issue, and a determined race between two athletes of the Apollo build, thrilled the blood and made people tingle with excitement. Some fifteen yards from the tape Stevenson got on terms with the Cantab. They raced stride by stride, but Stevenson had just the more reserve of stamina, and stretching for the worsted broke it inches in front of Butler, who may have lost these inches by once peer-

ing round. There is nothing like setting eyes on the goal and pressing forward for the prize.

Cecil Griffiths, Harold Abrahams (long jump), Eric Liddell (100 and 220 yards) and Henry Stallard (mile) were widely listed together in the press as champions, each for the first time. All were beginning to look like a good bet for the 1924 Olympic Games.

At the dinner given for the new champions and officials that evening, it was reported that Harry Barclay was full of praise:

> He [Barclay] remarked that records had been beaten that week in other parts of the world, but he did not think that one could have seen any finer performance than those that had been accomplished at Stamford Bridge that day.

Harold Abrahams' response to the Champions' Toast was liberally spiced with self-effacing humour:

> He [Abrahams] had always understood that Scotsmen were very close, but he now thought the trouble was that none of the Englishmen were close enough… he had hitherto associated Scotland with whisky and broth and Edinburgh in particular with rock. Now however, he was bound to associate Edinburgh with a whirlwind.

Abrahams' humour disguised his discomfort. The Edinburgh whirlwind was Eric Liddell. Abrahams had ambitions to compete in the sprints as well as the long jump, but was aware that his own pace was not adequate to match Liddell having been eliminated in the 100 yards and pulled out of the 220 yards after winning his heat. 'I don't run to take beatings. I run to win,' he is claimed to have said.

As a result of this perceived humiliation on the track, he approached Albert Hill for advice, asking him whether Polytechnic Harriers coach Sam Mussabini could help in any way. Mussabini thought he could find Abrahams a few yards in the sprints by improving his style and arm action to harness his nervous energy; from this a legendary partnership was formed. It was a controversial arrangement; there were many critics who objected to an amateur employing the services of a private professional coach.

There was a clear divide between the two social classes of competitor. For Abrahams there was no investigation or reprimand from the AAA for straying into the no man's land between amateurism and professionalism. They were far too class-bound to risk antagonising their own people who governed and drove forward athletics, perpetuating the state of affairs which favoured the privileged. It is highly unlikely an Achilles Club member like Abrahams was ever asked to lay bare the state of his bank account under the suspicion of professionalism. If working-class athletes like Cec or Albert Hill had treated themselves to the luxury of a personal trainer (not that they could have afforded it), Harry Barclay would soon have been knocking on their door demanding to know where they had got the money from.

Cec was one of the most celebrated and respected athletes in the country. This attracted the attention of Barclay, who was no stranger to Cec's home or the offices of Surrey AC and Ted Vowles in his quest to keep the sport amateur. On more than one occasion, Cec had to provide Barclay with a list of prizes in case they exceeded the limits set by the AAA and details of meetings attended to ensure his expenses didn't exceed income. Vowles was necessarily an expert at keeping on the right side of Barclay and ensured that he stayed at arm's length. Unfortunately he had not been so successful in ensuring that all his members were eligible for competition.

The lure of taking part in the fifth Triangular International Contest at Stoke football ground on 14 July 1923 was insufficient to steal Cec from competing in the Welsh Championship, a country without its own international athletics identity. As a proud Welshman, it was no surprise that he chose to entertain his own countrymen at Cardiff Arms Park, and he was well rewarded. So while Jack Gillis was emerging as the villain of the piece in Eric Liddell's heroic 440 yards recovery (he also won the 100 yards and 220 yards to give Scotland a narrow overall win), Cec easily took the double again in his favoured 880 yards and 440 yards. The organisers failed to advertise the event adequately which resulted in a low attendance, but Cec wasn't disappointed, especially when he saw the kind words and a cartoon of him in the *South Wales Echo*. There was further Welsh success when he lowered his own 880 yards Welsh record to 1:57.6 in an event at Rodney Parade, Newport on 6 August.

Aside from the races in the Welsh Championship, where there was a distinct lack of competition, Cec also continued to take part in the occasional 440 yards race elsewhere and proved that he still had the pace to win in a long sprint. One of these was the Kinnaird Trophy, where Cec broke the tape first in a close finish in which the first four were separated by two metres. Why Cec reverted to his old distance to allow Stallard a free reign in the half mile is unknown, but it provided his second win in the new annual contest.

Cec's successes brought him several accolades. He featured on a cigarette card in the Gallaher's British Champions of 1923 series, probably the ultimate recognition for a sportsman in the 1920s. Few families were without a smoker in their midst so the clumsily painted but colourful image of him, produced in vast quantities, made him a household name. Cec was also garnering an international reputation. The French magazine *Équipe* featured an iconic image of him running at full stretch, full-page and in colour, its purpose to analyse his long and graceful stride in conjunction with his arm action. The article confirmed the affection the French had held for Cec since he first competed there in 1921.

A light-hearted book of poems dedicated to Surrey AC members titled *Athletic Memories* by W.L. Heard captured the characters of the athletes and officials it targeted. Cec's standing within the club was acknowledged by his poem, the second of 29:

Cecil is a Welshman, and Wales no doubt is proud,
To honour his ability, and sing his praises loud;
An Athletic "Crack",
Who excels on the track,
And threatens all records to break;
The ease and the grace he displays in the race,
 Rank second only to his phenomenal pace,
To say he is "some" runner would make folks just laugh,
We are yearning for Cecil's best time in the half.

Heard, a previous Surrey champion suffering the bane of retired athletes, the indignity of unemployment, played on the sympathy vote to earn a few pence.

> Lack of employment for over a year has brought real poverty decidedly near.
> By asking all members to purchase a sheet, so that the writer and kiddies may eat.

The only member of Surrey AC to be given a higher billing than Cec in the book was the still-suspended Ted Vowles. His continuing absence was being felt by the club, and Cec was soon to feel that more than anybody.

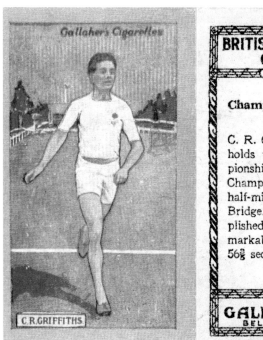

**BRITISH CHAMPIONS
OF 1923**

SERIES OF 75

**Champion Half-mile
Runner.**

C. R. Griffiths, of Neath,
holds the A. C. Cham-
pionship and A.A.A.
Championship for the
half-mile at Stamford
Bridge. He accom-
plished this in the re-
markable time of 1 min.
56$\frac{2}{5}$ secs.

72

ISSUED BY

GALLAHER LTD
BELFAST & LONDON.

C.R.GRIFFITHS.

The AAA Champion is commemorated
before his world falls apart

11

THE

FALL

1923-1924

On 23 July 1923, the Sixth Congress of the International Amateur Athletic Federation was held in Paris. Their President welcomed 27 council delegates representing sixteen countries, including Harry Barclay of the British AAA. Once the meeting was underway, Baron Pierre de Coubertin, the President of the IOC, was received as a guest amidst great applause. The minutes of this Congress make unremarkable reading, generally self-congratulatory and routine, until Article 10. This proposed an addition to the rules concerning amateur status.

The French delegates had requested a definition of the existing rules which governed whether professionals or semi-professionals could regain status as an amateur and take part in international meetings like the Olympics or Fraternité Cup. This had been prompted by AAA advice to British athletes not to compete against the French athlete, Jean Vermeulen, who the Fédération Française d'Athlétisme had reinstated as an amateur and allowed to compete internationally. Contrary to the situation in most countries, France had a professional athletics association and the FAA was trying to suppress it by encouraging former professionals like Vermeulen back into the amateur fold.

Recognising that their existing rules were open to misinterpretation regarding the reinstatement of professionals as amateurs, the IAAF President, Sigfrid Edstrom of Sweden, read a pre-prepared statement to the congress which explained the circumstances surrounding Vermeulen. It emphasised their philosophy that athletes who had violated the application of sporting regulations or circumvented the rules defining an amateur could not be allowed to regain status as an amateur 'regardless of by what method they have become professionals'. To make the matter perfectly clear the statement proposed the following rule be added to their section regarding amateur status:

> Anyone who shall have knowingly become a professional shall not be reinstated as an amateur.

The nature of the wording implied that there was no time limit as to how far back an athlete's career could be scrutinised in order to identify any misdemeanour. Mr Picot, one of the seven French delegates, demanded the proposition be amended to not have 'a retroactive effect'. Harry Barclay, the only representative from Britain, opposed this amendment. He specifically cited the case of Vermeulen and considered it unjust that a former professional might be allowed to compete at the Olympic Games.

Opinion was divided amongst the 27 council members. Even the French delegates were not in full agreement. Colonel Mills of the USA thought that the word 'knowingly' suppressed the possibility of injustice being done towards athletes who had violated amateur status inadvertently. The debate raged all morning and a break was called for lunch, during which heated words were exchanged over champagne and caviar. Barclay and the posse of French officials were the most vociferous in voicing their opinions.

Whatever was discussed during those two off the record hours brought the matter to a swift conclusion. When they resumed, Mr Genet, one of the French rebels, proposed the congress vote to adopt the amendment as originally proposed without modification, but including further explanation:

> Anyone who shall have knowingly become a professional shall not be reinstated as an amateur. This addition not being a modification of the Amateur Status but only a more definite interpretation of the text. It is understood that the International Federation will only recognise as an amateur an athlete who has always satisfied the above obligation.

This proposition was seconded by Mr Maccabe of the USA and Harry Barclay and its acceptance was passed unanimously. Barclay would return to England with the means to exclude any athlete who had in the past contravened amateur status.

Before Barclay crossed the Channel, he enjoyed the sights of Paris for a few days. Six days after the IAAF Congress, Cec and his English teammates joined him to compete in the Pershing Stadium on 29 July for the Fraternité Cup, the annual England v France international. In the 400 metres he was beaten by his two friends Jack Gillis and Gaston Féry, but gained victory in his now-specialist 800 metres. It was another victory over Edgar Mountain and his time of 1:57.0 established the best time by a Welsh athlete at this metric distance, a performance that stood for six years.

Cec had contributed to the overall English victory, 69 points to 42. It was fortunate that England won every track event because they lost all of field events except the hammer, in which M.C. Nokes threw a massive 173 feet 1 inch, nearly fifty feet further than the second-placed effort. Commentators considered the general standard of British field event athletes to be appalling and blamed it on the more glamorous track events attracting the bulk of interest.

The presentation of the Fraternité Cup was made after the day's competition at a banquet laid on by the FAA and attended by many members of the French government. As usual, Cec passed around his menu for all to sign which resulted in an eclectic mix of names from the worlds of international athletics and politics. One of those who added their signature was Eddie Owen, who was representing the AAA with Harry Barclay. Owen had won a silver medal in the five miles at the 1908 London Olympics and a bronze in the team 3,000 metres at Stockholm in 1912. His 1914 British record for 1,000 metres would soon be the focus of Cec's attention.

On 11 August 1923, Cec competed in the half mile handicap at the Glasgow Celtic Sports, entertaining the crowds with a fast but unchallenged win in the 880 yards which was reported by the *Daily Record* as the 'feature of the meeting'. It was only 0.6 seconds slower than his personal best at Herne Hill a year earlier, the best ever by a Welsh athlete, and many conjectured whether the British record might have been broken if Cec had been pressed. He admitted afterwards that if he had known he was so close, he would have made the extra effort. The cutting from the *Daily Record* described him as 'a lovely runner… and from an aesthetic point of view was an 880 artist'. Jack Gillis had a poor showing in the quarter mile and the newspaper explained, 'He had a very swollen toe, so we are informed, and could not in consequence do himself justice... A friend of his asks us to make mention of this fact.' The anonymous informant was undoubtedly Cec.

It was not all major championships and record attempts. For several years Cec competed at the annual Crittall's Sports meeting at the firm's ground in Braintree. The handicappers there never did top athletes like Cec any favours and the event in 1923 was no exception. Starting on scratch with considerable distances given to the other runners, Cec only came second in the 440 yards. However, he wasn't competing seriously; he was there to enjoy the day with the crowds who poured into the ground in their thousands. The venue had been decorated with flags and bunting in the blue and yellow colours of the steel windows firm. To add to the carnival atmosphere a ladies' rest tent was provided and a regimental band played, and there were competitions for cycling, poultry, other animals and horticulture. It was the only event at which Cec's name was ever listed alongside the grower of the largest onion or the best ferret.

· This particular occasion would have been memorable for Cec because of an incident involving an old Army horse spooked by the band. The panicking beast ran amok through the crowd while pulling a cart and smashed through the wooden entrance gate as the police on duty tried to close it to contain the poor animal. It then attempted to jump a fence outside the ground with the cart still attached. Incredibly, the horse remained unscathed, which was more than could be said for the cart. The only injury sustained was to the brave man who managed to secure the frantic animal after its leap as it emerged disorientated from the spars of wood and splinters. He was taken to the local hospital by ambulance with broken bones protruding from his hand, injuries described as 'minor' by the *Chelmsford Chronicle*. The presentation dinner held that evening in the firm's canteen was a spirited affair with the hurdling horse's antics being one of the main topics of conversation.

The arrival of John made it necessary for the family to move from the house in Stratford which had been Cec's home in London since 1919 when he was taken in as a lodger. Cec's landlady, 'Nanny' Woodroffe, who was godmother to John, treated him like her own grandchild and was sorry to see them go. As they were only moving to a house a few yards down the road, she would still get plenty of chance to care for the baby. On one occasion she took John out in his pram and encountered a German brass band marching through the East End streets. She was reportedly amazed to see him, just a baby, tapping out the rhythm of the music with his fingers on the side of the pram. It's surely a family myth, but John did grow up to have a love of music.

Cec was enjoying the high point of his life. He was a continuing success in athletics, leading to increased fame and becoming a favourite for the 800 metres at the next year's Olympic Games. Fatherhood had brought his loving relationship with May even closer. Yet, unknown to Cec and May, the lowest point of his running career was just around the corner.

The AAA General Committee met at the Stadium Club, High Holborn on 28 September 1923, instead of their usual Adelphi offices in London. The main topic on the agenda was the resolution agreed at the IAAF Congress on 23 July in Paris regarding amateur status. Unopposed, it was incorporated into AAA rules with only minor grammatical amendments. A separate committee, unnamed in the minutes of the General Committee, was appointed to consider the position, report upon the matter and decide the best method of dealing with it. This sub-committee was to be made up of Harry Barclay, the executive officers of the AAA and two representatives from each district.

At the same meeting, a letter was produced from Surrey AC with reference to the suspension of Ted Vowles by the Southern Committee and requesting his reinstatement. The

General Committee's response was to pass another resolution confirming their unwillingness to alter or amend the previous decision, leaving Vowles impotent as far as running his own club was concerned and straight-jacketed when it came to helping Cec deflect the storm soon to overwhelm him.

Then it came, out of nowhere, a lightning bolt that shocked the British athletics community to its core. The AAA announced that, subsequent to a ruling from the IAAF, Cecil Griffiths' status as an amateur had been revoked. In effect, Cec was banned from all amateur athletics events, both home and abroad.

*

The reason given for Cec's ban was that, as a youth, he had taken part and won prize money in an unregistered race in which professionals had competed. This information was widely reported by the contemporary press but the AAA never divulged the detail of his crime.

For Cec's story to be accurately told, it is essential that the race or races that caused him to be banned are identified. This proved no easy affair, consuming many hours of research and miles on the road in my VW Campervan. These races were outside the auspices of the AAA so they held no records, as was the case with Welsh Athletics.

IAAF rules only applied to athletes once they reached the age of sixteen. The wording of Cec's ban described him as a youth, so he must have run as a professional in a race before he was eighteen, when he moved to London to run for the Army.

Family history only provided a few clues and the information provided by Cec himself was vague and misleading. He later referred to his ban, saying, 'They had raked up some of my past career and found that I had competed with "pros" at Pontardawe and other sports meetings round there.'

Local historians and press gave no solid clues to identify an athletics track or any race meetings at Pontardawe, a small town six miles north of Neath. All circumstantial evidence suggests that athletics meetings would have been held on the Recreation Ground, the home of Pontardawe RFC. The sports field was a stunning location, wedged between the River Tawe and the Swansea Canal, overlooked by wooded hillside to the east and west of the valley. It remains mostly unchanged, unblemished by development, and if Cec ever did race there, it is another location he would instantly recognise today. However, there was no record of Cec competing in any races, although it is entirely feasible that Cec referred to an unidentified race.

Confident the location had been found and knowing that wartime sporting events were strenuously advertised and reported, it remained a straightforward but onerous task to examine contemporary newspapers for information. To this end I practically took up residence at Neath Library for several days scrolling through their microfiche records of the local papers for the period 1915 to 1917, but the only sporting events held at Pontardawe appeared to be for boxing and horse racing.

South Wales was devoid of carnivals involving sport during 1916 as the war consumed all human endeavour and the newspapers concentrated on the ebb and flow of the global conflict. However, a change in Glamorgan's mood was evident in 1917, possibly influenced by America's entry into the war in April which encouraged an optimistic mood, manifesting itself in a resurgence of charity sports events throughout South Wales. Widening the search area, a flurry of notices advertising carnivals throughout Carmarthenshire, Gwent and Glamorgan invited entries for a variety of races at Llanelly, Newport, Aberpergwm and Gorseinon. The results were duly reported in the press but there was no mention of a young Cecil Griffiths at any of them. Within a year he would make a major impact on military athletics, so if he had been active in local, low-key competitions, surely he would have featured in the results.

Hopes of finding him in a race, either at Pontardawe or anywhere else, receded as 1917 wore on. Then, beyond all hope and expectation, his name headed the results in a 440 yards open handicap in the grounds of Neath Abbey on 28 July. It was like glimpsing an apparition; the ghost of Cecil Griffiths shrouded in the fog of a grey computer screen. It was unbelievable, requiring several blinks of the eye to retain focus and convince the mind it wasn't boggled by the long hours of concentration staring into the ether.

Every one of his press cuttings in my possession was from a later period and had been handed down through the family, but this was self-discovered; the proverbial 'eureka' moment which prompted a loud exclamation of emotion in the hushed library. The Olympic relay win was the second race to shape his destiny. Was this the first, alluded to in almost every subsequent article written about him? Nobody has ever publicly identified it and few have probably cast eyes on the race report concealed in the *South Wales Daily Post* for nearly a century. The excitement at finding this deeply hidden and elusive information was even greater than, as an underwater archaeologist, my first discovery of *Mary Rose*'s timbers concealed under deep layers of Solent silt for 450 years.

What now appears likely is that Cec had been discovered to have accepted prize money at three races in 1917. One was held at Neath Abbey where he won £3, one at Victoria Park in Swansea where he won prizes of £1 and £3 very publicly in front of a massive crowd, and one at The Gnoll where the prize is unknown. Just to take part in an unregistered race, let alone win money, would have been a dangerous folly for anyone with an ambition to make a career in amateur athletics. However, Cec was naïve, if not ignorant, regarding the politics and pitfalls associated with the cash he took home. In the grand scheme of things it was not a great amount, but it was certainly sufficient to perk the interest of the AAA when the time came.

When Cec took his marks on those three race tracks, his youthful innocence would have prevented him from realising his actions would jeopardise his future in athletics. He measured his future in terms of days and weeks. If young Cec had been asked where he would be in six years time, he would probably have answered that he would be still working and living in Neath, not an Olympic and AAA Champion.

For a seventeen-year-old boy, it was a rare chance to enjoy a bit of sport in support of a good cause, with the prospect of a cash prize acting as a secondary motive. There were no alternative events for him to compete in and the last thing on his mind would have been the ethical maze of taking a prize for running.

Cec would have been ignorant of the strict amateur code fiercely enforced by the AAA, an organisation he probably had never heard of, whose rules made it much easier for wealthy athletes with private means to succeed than working class ones who had to earn a living to stay alive and fund their involvement in the sport. Running and rugby were just a physical pleasure; a competitive stimulus not taken too seriously in view of the war raging around the world and the poverty of his family.

What remains unexplained is why Cec wrongly ascribed his ban to races around Pontardawe. It is possible he was fiercely protective of Neath and unwilling to darken the town's name by associating it with his ban. He was also aware that the race at Neath Abbey was sponsored by his uncle, William Trick, who may have persuaded Cec to run in the fateful race. It would hardly be surprising that Cec would not want to drag the name of his now-deceased uncle who had provided him with such opportunities in life, into the controversy.*

*

In the absence of any existing documents, how or when Cec was informed of the ban are not known. Cec's ban may have originated with the IAAF – they certainly involved themselves in the banning of individual athletes in the next

---

* Cec's son, John, would never hear a bad word against Neath and was adamant that a neighbouring town was to blame for what happened to his father, betraying the old rivalry which still exists between such communities. He was crestfallen when irrefutable evidence about his father's indiscretion could be attributed to a race in his home town.

decade – or it might have originated within the AAA itself, acting in response to the IAAF rule modification. Regrettably, an exhaustive search of AAA documents held in the Cadbury Research Library at Birmingham University, assisted by an enthusiastic and skilled team of professional archivists, reveals very little relevant information. The minutes of the unnamed committee set up at the General Committee meeting on 28 September to deal with the IAAF ruling on amateur status are not held, if they ever existed, and its report back to the General Committee is not reflected in their comprehensive minutes prior to Cec's ban. Whether any other athletes were subject to the mystery committee's attention or Barclay manipulated its formation just for the purpose of revealing information he held on Cec is unknown.

What is remarkable is the fact that one of the country's leading athletes – an Olympic gold medal winner – was banned, yet there is no record of it in any of the documents or annual reports belonging to the athletics authority of his country. The obvious conclusion is that Harry Barclay managed to administer the process of the ban in an unrecorded manner. However, it is also possible that the relevant documents are missing. When the AAA documents were first housed in the National Centre for Athletics Literature in the 1970s, several researchers decided to walk away with items. It is now housed under much higher security.

Whoever was responsible for instigating the ban and however it was put into practice, Cec was made aware of it sometime between September 1923 and 1924. AAA decisions were made in the public domain, so Cec may not even have been given the courtesy of a letter – certainly one was not retained with his other personal papers.

The minutes of the General Committee of the AAA show that they were very practised at suspending athletes on the home front. Their rules specified that an individual must be notified immediately after a sentence had been passed and their club must be made aware within seven days. No AAA committee recorded such action being taken regarding Cec, although the administration of an international ban was unfamiliar ground for them.

The wording of the IAAF regulation, stating that an athlete had to 'knowingly' become a professional, provided a defence to contest the ruling. It is inconceivable that somebody within the AAA didn't take up his case as soon as his career was jeopardised, but like lap dogs led by Barclay, they were submissive and hit him with the ban. There appears to have been no desire to find a solution to the problem. There is certainly no record of any debate on the subject of Cec's ban and reinstatement within the files of the AAA.

There must have been some dissent or unease amongst the committee members of the AAA because they refused to apply the ruling to Cec in national events. Presumably due to the 'special circumstances' in accordance with their own resolution agreed at the 1919 Annual General Meeting, Cec was reinstated as an amateur, which allowed him to continue entertaining UK crowds competing as a reinstated professional. However, as a reinstated professional he could only compete *in* Great Britain, not *for* Great Britain. Cec was one of the country's best athletes, a near certainty for a medal at the next Olympic Games. Now, he would not be able to compete.

It was a grossly unfair situation, the core of which came down to how men like Cec suffered as a consequence of their place in society. The upper classes dominated the administration of athletics and it would be against human nature if they didn't look after their own. The members of Achilles Club – those from Oxford and Cambridge Universities – were the preferred breeding ground for top quality athletes. Working-class athletes like Cec who came from the grass roots of the sport were not part of their circle. Once the finger was pointed at Cec, they had no real reason to fight his corner. In addition, there were undoubtedly many individuals on the various committees of the AAA who were class-prejudiced and would have been conspiring to eliminate Cec from the ranks of the crack athletes to allow their own members, especially Achilles, a free reign.

The only link between the IAAF meeting that agreed the rule modification and the AAA General and Special Committees was Harry Barclay, a man with bulldog tenacity. From the day Barclay walked out of the IAAF meeting in July that year, it was a done deal. Barclay would not have been driven by a desire to cleanse the sport of the working classes. The various offices he held in athletic clubs before he became Secretary of the AAA in 1915 suggests he came up through the grass roots of club competition rather than through the varsity system. Perhaps he was overzealous in protecting an archaic ideal of the amateur status. For years, he had been pursuing working-class athletes like Cec and Albert Hill, poring over their paperwork with a suspicious eye.

Perhaps Barclay's objection to Cec being picked for the 1920 Olympic team stemmed back to information that he already had about Cec's past. He had made his objections to former professionals competing at the Olympic Games very clear at the 1923 IAAF Congress and he had followed through on those objections as soon as he got the chance.

If Barclay and the AAA could not be expected to fight for Cec, who could? It is hardly believable Cec's backers like Joe Binks and the Vowles family did not help him fight this travesty of justice. The timing of Ted Vowles' suspension, preventing him from taking part in the management of athletics, could not have been worse for Cec. His son, Cyril, had taken over the management of Surrey AC, but undoubtedly his father was still in control behind the scenes. Ted Vowles' suspension was lifted by the AAA shortly before the 1924 Olympic Games, but it was too late to campaign for Cec's international ban being lifted.

Officially there was no mechanism to appeal an IAAF decision, but if Cec or his advisers had been privy to the minutes of the IAAF meeting on 23 July 1923, he could have mounted a challenge based upon the wording of the rules regarding an athlete 'knowingly' becoming a professional. It was an argument not used in his defence, yet it was one which had been provided for exactly the situation he found himself in. It is unlikely any tribunal would have considered such small cash prizes awarded at a wartime charity carnival where other events included an obstacle race and a pillow fight, to a young lad who rarely competed, as being grounds for him knowingly competing as a professional.

Yet there is no evidence in the AAA archives of any challenge being made either by Cec or on his behalf, and there is no memory carried within the family to suggest it happened. Cec simply took it lying down, not wanting to make a fuss. That was his nature. Although he thought it extremely unfair, he knew the reason for the ban to be true. He had accepted money in wartime charity races, he could not deny it.

Cec never discovered where the information the IAAF or AAA acted upon came from. He suspected that Barclay was involved, still harbouring a grudge over being overruled on the subject of his and Albert's selection for the 1920 Olympics. If he had been aware of Barclay's declaration at the IAAF meeting that former professionals should never be allowed to compete at the Olympic Games, he would have been convinced. Cec also thought that the encounter with the mystery man at the event in 1917 had something to do with it. Was he one of Barclay's informers?

Cec beats a despairing Douglas Lowe in the Kinnaird Trophy. This victory against the soon-to-be Olympic Champion neatly illustrates the tragedy that Cec was denied his chance to claim the Olympic crown.

12

THE

COLLAPSE
1924

It was inevitable that the AAA would not consider Cec for the 1924 Olympic Games. The decision (unlike his initial ban or reason for it) was starkly recorded in the minutes of the AAA General Committee meeting on 6 May 1924:

> After serious and careful consideration it was decided with very great regret that the Committee was not in a position

to avail itself of the services of Mr C.R. Griffiths to represent Great Britain at the VIII Olympiad.

The news was devastating for Cec, causing him to plunge into misery. At the dawn of a new athletics season, an Olympic season, it was all suddenly very real. A.B. George wrote in *All Sports Weekly*:

> There is not the slightest doubt that Griffiths was materially affected by the news that the Amateur Athletic Association authorities did not feel justified in selecting him for the Olympic team of 1924. He collapsed when told this, and for weeks was positively ill in mind.

George was one of Cec's greatest allies in the athletics world and knew him well. His statement that Cec was 'ill in mind' suggests that Cec fell into some kind of depression – something that had previously affected him when he was waiting to be called up for the First World War. Whether he suffered full-blown depression or not is unclear, but what can be without doubt was that this was one of the lowest moments of his life.

There was no public pronunciation from Cec. Privately, in a letter to his mother, he complained bitterly about the way he had been treated and expressed his grievance over the unfair policies adopted by those who governed his sport. He couldn't understand why it was permissible for a student at Oxford or Cambridge to receive a generous allowance from wealthy parents to fund his athletics, whereas a boy from a struggling family could be outcast from the amateur ranks for accepting a small cash prize many years previously.

Cec had to get on with the athletics events that the AAA graciously allowed him to compete in. The 1924 Welsh Championship had been brought forward to 24 May, not that it mattered much to Wales' biggest star anymore. For the third consecutive year, at the peak of his career, he took the double in the 440 and 880 yards. Winning the double three times, let alone three years in a row, has not been achieved since. Even if it is, Cec's imperial record can never be eclipsed.*

The annual Kinnaird Trophy was also brought forward, to 31 May at Stamford Bridge. Cec and Douglas Lowe engaged in the closest half mile battle of their careers. The first lap was slow, with the field tightly bunched, but at the bell Lowe broke away, closely pursued by Cec. As they ran the back straight Lowe had a two-yard advantage, but doggedly, inch by inch, Cec reduced this to a foot as they entered the final bend. After a terrific neck-and-neck struggle down the straight, Cec broke the tape inches ahead of one of Great Britain's 800 metres Olympic contenders. The race was tactical; a first lap of 67.6 and a second one of 55.2, totalling 2:02.8. It was a classic example of Cec using his brain in conjunction with his scintillating speed to dumfound his rivals. *The Times* declared, 'The fact that Griffiths is debarred from competing in the Olympic Games robs Great Britain of the services of a great half-miler.' Certainly this race demonstrated that Cec was at least as good as the Olympic Champion in waiting.

* Only Jim Alford, who broke Cec's 880 yards Welsh record in 1934, has managed to win a 440/880 yard double since, in 1946. It has not been achieved at all in the metric 400/800 metres era.

Other athletes were reaching their peak during the Olympic Trials, but Cec's ban prevented him from entering those meetings and he lost motivation. That led to a poor result at the AAA Championship at Stamford Bridge on 21 June, when Cec was beaten into third place in the 880 yards. Henry Stallard and Douglas Lowe fought a close race and Cec trailed in some eight yards behind. Stallard was a mile specialist but came from nowhere to equal Frances Cross' 1888 British record time of 1:54.6, overtaken by Mel Sheppard in 1908.

Cec was probably unaware of the part his friend Albert Hill played in his defeat and Stallard's success. Stallard clearly had great respect for his old mile adversary and approached him for advice. Hill, now a part-time coach, was able to identify a fundamental fault which was affecting his balance. Stallard's arm action was asymmetric, creating an uneven stride – he would have been well advised to study Cec's style – and, without much effort, he was able to correct it. Albert also suggested a rest from competition and to try the half mile when he resumed; it was a package for which Stallard must have been eternally grateful and proof of Albert's potential to become an excellent coach.

Although Cec had lost his AAA Championship title in the individual 880 yards, the mile medley relay provided a consolation and harked back to 1922 with another win for the Surrey AC team, Cec once again setting them up on the all-important 880 yards first leg.

Cec may have lost a little motivation, but he was still capable of outstanding performances. At the 1924 London AC summer meeting on 28 June, Cec won the 600 yards in 1:12.2. Considering that he was running against an adverse wind and eased up at the end, it was only 1.2 seconds outside the British record. At this point in time, just a week before the English team left for Paris, Cec was back in dominant form and one can imagine the frustration he suffered at being left behind.

There is some suggestion that Cec travelled with the British Olympic team to Paris. This was improbable, although Cec might have hoped for a last-minute reprieve. Albert Hill had competed at Antwerp without attending the trials and there were even precedents where members of the crowd had stood in to fill vacancies at previous Olympics. It is possible, but unlikely, that representations were being undertaken on his behalf right until the eleventh hour. However, the AAA would not have condoned or financed his involvement with the team; after all, it was they who had decided not to select him following the IAAF ruling which instigated his ban.

For the second Olympic Games in a row, Cec's dreams of competing in an individual event were dashed. On 8 July, the 800 metres went ahead in the Stade Colombes without him. Cec was upset that his good friend Edgar Mountain, who had dominated 880 yards races between 1921 and 1923, did not qualify for the 800 metres final. His ranking as a middle-distance runner was slipping and the Olympics would be his swan song. The siren of his profession, the Achilles heel of Achilles Club members, was calling.[*]

The winner of the close contest was the new Brit on the block, Douglas Lowe, with Paul Martin of Switzerland fin-

***

[*] Although Achilles claim Edgar Mountain's successes as their own on their website, he in fact won those titles as a member of Surrey AC or Cambridge University AC.

ishing second, a tenth of a second behind. New half miler Henry Stallard was fourth, recording the same time as Schuyler, the American in third place. Lowe's winning time was only half a second outside the world record set by Ted Meredith at Stockholm twelve years earlier.

No eligible athlete in the world could match Lowe on the day – but perhaps Cec could have. Cec had beaten the new Olympic Champion in the Kinnaird Trophy a few weeks previously. He had beaten the silver medallist, Paul Martin of Switzerland, in the 880 yards at the 1922 AAA Championship. Cec would clearly have been a strong contender for a medal, and who knows, maybe he could have upped his game like Lowe and Martin and won gold.*

There were other British successes at the 1924 Games which have gone down as some of the most famous and memorable in history. The day before the 800 metres, 7 July, Harold Abrahams won the 100 metres. His coach, Sam Mussabini, didn't have the pleasure of witnessing it because his status as a professional barred him entry to Stade Colombes. He stayed in a hotel within sight of the stadium and, at 7 o'clock, listened as the noise generated by the crowd intensified to a crescendo as the finalists sped along the red clay towards the line. Mussabini sensed it had been close, and being able to see the top of the flagpole from his room, watched in hopeful anticipation for the victor's flag to be raised. When he saw the Union Jack flutter its way aloft to unfurl in glory as the band played the National Anthem, the film *Chariots of Fire* would like us to believe that Mussabini

* Clive Williams, noted historian of Welsh athletics, also believes Cec was passed over by history. In an exchange of emails discussing the subject he wrote, 'There is absolutely no doubt in my mind had Cec been in Paris he would have won a medal.'

took off his straw boater in respect and stood stunned for a moment before sitting on the bed where he punched his fist through the hat in joy. Arthur Porritt, a New Zealander and Abraham's fellow member of Achilles, came third. From that day, they organised their lives so that every year on 7 July at 7 o'clock they dined together.

The day after the 800 metres final, in the same stadium where he made his international rugby debut in 1922, Eric Liddell won a bronze medal in the 200 metres. It must have felt like a consolation prize; he had failed in his favoured event. Three days later he received his just reward in the 400 metres, an unfamiliar event which he was not expected to win. Running it like a sprint in his inimitable style, head up looking to Heaven, the devout Christian won it in the Olympic record time of 47.6 seconds. Guy Butler was third.

The following day, Henry Stallard won bronze in the 1,500 metres, running without painkillers despite a stress fracture in his foot. His time of 3:55.6 was the fastest ever recorded by a British athlete. Paavo Nurmi won the race, setting a new Olympic record of 3:53.6. 45 minutes later, Nurmi started the 5,000 metres. He won a second Olympic title in the course of an hour in another Olympic record time of 14:31.2. By also winning the individual cross-country, team cross-country and the team 3,000 metres, his five gold medals took his total tally of Olympic titles to eight. He would win another gold medal and three silver medals in 1928 at Amsterdam to leave no doubt that he had fulfilled Cec's 1920 prediction that he would 'do great things'.

On 13 July, the last day of athletics competition, Harold Abrahams won a silver medal in the 4x100 metres relay. It was a close race with the Americans lowering the world record they had set at Antwerp in 1920, but they needed to do so – the runners-up also ran one second inside the old record.

In the last event of the athletics, the 4x400 metres relay, the two men who *Athletic News* had described at the 1923 AAA Championship as being of 'Apollo build, big enough to eat their foes', faced each other for their mightiest mortal challenge. Guy Butler and Bill Stevenson were the most experienced men in the British and USA relay teams, but they ran different legs so they didn't get the chance for a rematch. The closely-contested race was won by the USA in a world record time of 3:16.0 with Sweden one second behind. Guy Butler, on the anchor leg as usual, brought his team home in an unexpected third place, their time of 3:17.4 being the fastest ever for a British team.

Were it not for the ban, Cec would certainly have been in the team with Guy Butler in an attempt to repeat their Antwerp success together. Although he was no longer a 400 metres specialist, he had a reputation as an excellent relay runner and had far better form than the other three medallists; Edward Toms, Richard Ripley and George Renwick. It was widely believed if he or Liddell (who declined to race in the relays because they were on a Sunday) had been involved, the world record and victory may well have been within their grasp.

Guy Butler's two medals at Paris took his Olympic tally to four, not beaten to this day by any British track and field athlete. It was equalled by Sebastian Coe with a gold and silver at Moscow in 1980, a feat he repeated at Los Angeles in 1984. Fate plays a part in every life, but it had been particularly cruel to Cec – if he had not been ill in Antwerp and if he had not been banned from Paris, he may have shared that honour with Butler and Coe.

Abrahams and Liddell returned to England with two medals each; the sum total of their Olympic efforts as both of their careers would end the following year. In 1925, Abrahams broke his leg while demonstrating long jump technique to the press and Liddell departed for China to continue his family's missionary work. Both spent a relatively short time of their lives fulfilling their athletics aspirations but both brought great credit to Great Britain and themselves in the manner they achieved it.

Cec was robbed of the opportunity to win further Olympic glory. His so-called professionalism and the few pounds prize money he received had not contributed to his success as an amateur. On the other hand, Abrahams had employed the services of a professional coach, Sam Mussabini, which unarguably improved his ability when comparing his results in the 1923 AAA Championship to the 1924 Olympics. Hypocrisy, inconsistency, unfairness, class and education were all factors involved when the governing bodies of athletics made their decisions about the treatment of professionalism. Abrahams predictably fared much better than Cec.

Cec's despondency was compounded by his exclusion from the second British Empire Meeting at Stamford Bridge on 19 July, a contest between the British Empire and the returning USA Olympic team. With a crowd of 40,000, this was one of the best attended athletics meetings ever held in Great Britain, but Cec was unable to share the excitement and contribute to the efforts of the three relay teams. Two were successful; Liddell joined up with three of the 4x400 metres bronze medal Olympians; Edward Toms, Richard Ripley and Guy Butler, for the 4x440 yards relay, beating the victorious American Olympians in 3:18.2 to break the British record set at the same meeting in 1920 by Cec and his Surrey AC colleagues. In the 4x880 yards event, Edgar Mountain, Clarence Oldfield, Harry Houghton and Henry Stallard also triumphed. The mile medley relay team consisting of Eric Liddell, Arthur Porritt, Guy Butler and Douglas Lowe nearly made it a clean sweep for the track relays but lost by just a foot to the Americans.

Olympic medals were being won and records were being broken. One can only imagine the heartache Cec suffered as a result of being unable to be involved. It would have been natural for him to have become embittered, but he maintained his dignity and did not make any criticism in public about his treatment. He still had his family, his health and his job. At least he could still compete in domestic events and thrill the large enthusiastic crowds which they attracted.

On 26 July, eighteen days after the 800 metres Olympic final, the Essex Championship was held on Brentford School grounds for the first time. Cec won his third consecutive half mile title in a time of 1:56.4. Even though the grass track was wet and slippery he lowered the meeting record by eight seconds and helped Southend Harriers to a win in the mile relay with Jack Gillis and William Hill; E.R. Barber was the necessary non-Surrey AC man on this occasion.

On 2 August he won the half mile at the Glasgow Rangers Sports at Ibrox Park. The stadium could hold 40,000 and over the years Cec entertained a considerable number of Scots with his regular appearances. In gratitude, the Lord Provost of Glasgow, Sir Matthew Walker Montgomery, invited Cec to a private lunch with him in his room at the City Chambers on 5 August. The invitation card was luxurious and lavish – no doubt the lunch was the same.

A seemingly-minor race at Fallowfield near Manchester on 16 August 1924 was remembered by Cec as one of his best. He won a thrilling half mile handicap off scratch by one yard from an Irishman, G. Magan, who had been given 27 yards and a Scot, T.M. Riddell, who had a 30-yard start. *Athletic News* described it as 'a race which will live in one's memory'. Cec's winning time of 1:54.6 equalled Francis Cross's 1888 old British record, a time which Henry Stallard had also equalled at the AAA Championship two months earlier.

Stallard was subsequently credited with equalling Cross' English record in AAA Championship programmes, defined as the 'best performance by British athlete'. It was a confusing title born from necessity because it couldn't be called the British record. It was an unofficial guide for spectators to appreciate the performances of British athletes in Britain and a sign that the authorities were beginning to recognise that the system of monitoring records was no longer fit for purpose. However, Cec's identical time was not recognised and appears to have gone unnoticed by the authorities. Cec's Welsh nationality was not the problem, because there were Irish and Scottish athletes who held the English record for other disciplines. Fallowfield was a sanctioned venue; the inaugural English Championship was held there in 1923.

Several records had been ratified when an athlete started from scratch in a handicap race; Albert Hill had done so in 1919 at Glasgow when he equalled the British record at the Celtic Sports. Why Cec's time was never recognised as a joint English record is a mystery, but it may simply be that the unofficial nature of the record made it less formal and not all performances outside of the AAA Championships were identified.

Neath Cricket Club organised a three-day summer carnival in the town, the highlight being the inter-schools sports contest which over a thousand entered. Cec, described in the South Wales press as 'a record breaker and British representative at the Olympic Games', was there to present a cup in his name to the boy from his old school who scored the most points.

Cec may have been banned from representing Britain in international competition, but that did not prevent him from competing abroad. He was billed as the main attraction for the Trustens Internationella Idrottsfest in Stockholm at the end of September 1924.*

It was most unusual for a British athlete to go off on his own to compete abroad when not part of an official British team. But go off on his own was exactly what Cec did. Clearly his ban was not enforceable regarding individual appearances, nevertheless Cec was treading new ground and risking further displeasure from the AAA whose rules required an

---

* During a loft clearance, some old school exercise books of my brother-in-law and Cec's grandson, Nicholas, were discovered which hadn't seen the light of day for over forty years. One of them was a project on the Olympic Games and clearly he had used material from his grandfather's collection of memorabilia. Stuck to one of the pages was a leaflet in Swedish, a promotional flyer for an athletics event with Cec's picture on it. It was this that led to the discovery of Cec's Stockholm adventure.

athlete to seek their permission to do such a thing – there is no evidence that this occurred. A Swedish press cutting described his arrival at Stockholm harbour. The reporter was waiting dockside as the SS *Patricia* berthed. He was looking at the faces hanging over the rail trying to see a slightly-built 24-year-old runner, who the reporter considered very young for such a venture. After Cec disembarked, the reporter interviewed him as they walked to the station and noted his long, purposeful stride despite carrying a large suitcase. Cec talked to him about the beauty of Wales, being happily married and having a young son. At the station the reporter treated him to breakfast and Cec expressed his gratitude for Sweden's hospitality. There were no other British athletes present and clearly he was the guest of honour.

There was no likelihood of the AAA supporting or even condoning this trip, even without his ban. An invitation to Albert Hill and Harry Edward to compete in Sweden in 1921 had been politely but quickly declined on their behalf by the AAA.

Cec could not have afforded to finance the trip and the AAA would not have, so the Swedes must have sponsored his attendance. We shall never know for sure what brought the gifted young Welsh athlete so far from his home, but Cec certainly had the opportunity to forge links with Swedish athletes. He was known to form strong friendships with foreign runners – Gaston Féry of France was a particular friend – and would have met Swedish athletes at the 1920 Olympics, notably Nils Engdahl in the 4x400 metres relay final. Engdahl had also run alongside Cec at the 1919 AAA Championship when they came second and third in the 440 yards. Cec would also have had the opportunity to meet distance runner Sven Lundgren, who competed in the AAA Championship in 1921 at which Swedish athletes won the pole vault, triple jump, shot, discus, hammer and javelin, and the Crown Prince of Sweden was a VIP spectator.

Cec competed in three races. On 21 September he was third in a slow 880 yards with 2:00.3, only a second covering the first three. Considering that the pre-race publicity to draw in the Swedish crowd suggested Cec might break the world record for the 880 yards (1:52.2, set in 1912 by Ted Meredith in Philadelphia), it was a disappointing result. It was just desserts for the Swedish ad man who designed the publicity, plastering across the posters that Cec's best time was 1:52.4. Cec had no idea where they had plucked that figure from. The next day, he was fourth with 52.1 in the 440 yards won by Nils Engdahl in 49.4. The star attraction had done little to justify top billing.

Perhaps Cec was saving himself for the last day of competition. On 23 September, he was second in the 1,000 metres in 2:33.6, just 0.2 seconds behind Sven Lundgren, the Swedish world record holder, and four seconds ahead of René Wiriath, a finalist in the 1,500 metres at the Paris Olympics.

It was an unfamiliar distance, but Cec's time was the best ever by a British athlete, although it did not supersede Edward Owen's time of 2:35.2 as a British record because it was set outside Britain. Moreover, only first-place finishers were officially timed. However, it was one of Cec's greatest runs and he returned home with a pewter tray and a delicate bronze tablet to remind him of the occasion.

Cec's performances in 1924 illustrated that the Olympics had been robbed of a top athlete. In *All Sports Weekly*, A. B. George lamented Cec's disappointment over his non-selection for the Olympic team for 1924, reminding readers what a big part he had played in victory for the British team in the 4x400 metres relay race at the 1920 Olympic Games. However, George also looked to the positives and described the 'unbounded pleasure' Cec had given with his many victories. Above a familiar photograph of him running at full stride, the article was titled 'The Best Runner Wales Has Produced'. That label could still be argued today.

C. R. GRIFFITHS

Is one of the finest half-milers Great Britain has produced. For a long time he has been expected to create a new British record for the distance. It has been observed that he has been developing late this season and, given satisfactory conditions, the possibility has been canvassed of him putting up a particularly fast time to-day.

He is A.A.A. and Southern and Essex County half-mile champion.

When a youth he ran in some unregistered events and because of this was debarred by the International definition of an amateur from representing Great Britain in the last Olympic Games at Colombes, Paris.

He runs his halves with careful judgment, finding that a fairly fast first lap suits him as he is possessed of great stamina and can put up a determined finish after the most gruelling race.

Cec's profile shows him to be a big draw at Fallowfield

13

HOME IS WHERE THE HEART IS
1925

By the mid-1920s, Cec was certainly a nationally-recognised athlete. On Easter Sunday, 18 April 1925, he was due to take part in the *News of the World* London to Brighton relay race in which ten runners from each team ran four or five miles each. The newspaper covered a variety of sporting events that holiday weekend and for publicity purposes they featured a cartoon including well-known names from each of the sports. Cec was honoured to represent athletics; alongside new land speed record holder Malcolm Campbell (motor racing at Brooklands), Tom Newman (billiards), Billy Gillespie of Sheffield United (football) and Frank Bollock (horse racing at Kempton). Cec's face must have helped to attract the massive crowd which thronged the route of the race won by Birchfield Harriers. However, Cec's participation was wishful thinking on the part of the *News of the World* – he was not a member of the third-placed Surrey AC team and would not make his debut in the race for another three years.

The Essex Championship was held on 6 June on Crittalls Ground, Braintree in the presence of Harry Barclay. Cec's form indicated another record-breaking year was in the offing. The report of the meeting in the *Chelmsford Chronicle* suggests an element of showmanship to entertain the crowd of 6,000, most out of character for the usually-meek Cec. In the half mile he trailed the whole field for most of the race but, with a third of a lap to go, made 'a splendid spurt' to win by ten yards. Then in the 1,000 yards open handicap, starting on scratch, he overtook all thirty competitors 'in a splendid effort' for a comfortable win.

At the customary competitors' dinner and dance in the evening, Cec's gracious response to the Champions' Toast was that, 'Wherever the Championships were held, the same spirit of comradeship prevailed'. Perhaps he looked towards Barclay when he uttered those words, hoping to probe his thoughts and spot a pang of guilt. The AAA had not shown Cec any spirit of comradeship.

On 20 June Cec took his second AAA Southern Counties title in the half mile at Southend and a week later he attempted to beat Sven Lundgren's 1,000 metres world record in the London AC summer meeting at Stamford Bridge. Having beaten the British record time in Sweden the previous year, Cec had been persuaded to try again on home soil in conditions that would provide a ratified record. Cec started on scratch in a handicap race on a specially-measured metric track and utilising pacemakers. Pacemakers were illegal under AAA rules, but that law could be circumnavigated so long as it was not admitted and the pacemakers finished the race. They did – but in doing so, R. Downie, off 10 yards, beat Cec by inches on the soft track affected by heavy rain.

Cec's time of 2:31.8 was 3.2 seconds outside the ambitious world record target but 3.4 seconds inside Edward Owen's British record. Nevertheless, he could not claim it. Cec did not win so his second-place time was not official. Neither could Downie, as he had not started from scratch.

On 10 July, the day before the sixth Triangular International Contest at Croke Park in Belfast, the Scottish press let slip that they were running scared, fearing another beating by the English in the annual event. A misinformed, desperate and outspoken article in the *Evening Telegraph* titled 'Griffiths Mystery' demonstrated a level of resentment and sour grapes:

> The half-mile looks good for England with C.R. Griffiths taking part – yet one asks why, since Griffiths is Welsh and ineligible to compete in the English Championship?

They had a point of sorts. All the nations of the United Kingdom held their own national championships, and Cec enjoyed a great deal of success in the Welsh Championship. However, Wales did not have a recognised international identity and their athletes competed under England's banner until 1948. Considering that the combined population of England and Wales in 1925 was nearly forty million while Scotland and Ireland each had less than five million, the English/Welsh coalition made the outcome of the annual Triangular International nearly a foregone conclusion. Only exceptional circumstances would influence the result in Scotland's favour, as in 1921 when most of the English cracks stayed away because of the unrest in Belfast and 1923 when Eric Liddell virtually single-handedly carried the Scots to victory by winning three events.

Scotland's objection to Cec competing for England may have been more credible if they based it on his international ban. The AAA didn't classify the Triangular Contests as internationals because they were for the home nations only, but the Scots would have had a more powerful moral argument. Cec was probably glad that they didn't raise that issue.

England did indeed win, but in the half mile Ireland's Norman McEachern beat Cec by a few inches with a time of 1:58.4. McEachern was an Olympic semi-finalist in the 800 metres at the 1924 Olympics and would repeat that achievement at Amsterdam in 1928, but Cec was disappointed not to beat a man he was expected to.

The Welsh identity that the Scots had pointed out in the lead up to the Triangular International was the cause of a dilemma shortly afterwards – the AAA Championship clashed with the Welsh Championship. Cec plumped for the harder option of fighting for the AAA British title rather than the easier Welsh title, although it brought to an end Cec's run of five consecutive Welsh titles in the 440 yards and three in the 880 yards. The Welsh press were incensed they would be deprived of their champion at Pontypool Park, complaining vociferously about the lack of liaison between the English and Welsh authorities.

It was something of a gamble. Winning an AAA Championship event was a much taller order. The presence of Norman McEachern gave Cec a chance to avenge his defeat in Ireland the previous week.

From the gun, Cec went for the lead and kept to the inside for the very slow first lap, McEachern constantly at his shoulder, neither wishing to force the pace. At the bell, the field was bunched together. McEachern made his move, matched by Ray Dodge, an American invitee from Illinois AC. They raced stride for stride around the bend and along the back straight with Sydney Spencer following them closely behind. Cec remained focused, keeping in touch with the leading threesome, and jumped them coming off the last bend. A scintillating burst of acceleration saw him break free from the pack and he eased up to win by four yards from another strong finisher, William Nelson of Salford Harriers, who had shadowed him right round the last lap. Dodge held on to third place. As the *Sporting Life and Sportsman* reported, there was little doubt that Cec had 'very decisively atoned for his beating by McEachern last week'.

Cec's race tactics to become AAA Champion for the second time were a carbon-copy of the first occasion in 1923. His sprint finish had become a well-established and successful trademark since changing to the half mile. The 15 carat gold medal was a handsome addition to his six previous AAA medals.

Cec's gamble to miss the Welsh Championship had paid off handsomely and Wales rejoiced. The *South Wales Echo* sang his praises, explaining, 'It is but rarely that Welsh athletes become world-beaters, and the performances of the Neath athlete at Stamford Bridge was worthy of all the prominence it could be given.'

In the mile medley relay Cec gave the Surrey AC team a commanding lead on his 880 yards opening leg and Lancelot Royle increased it to a thirty yards but the other two runners, T. Matthewman and J. Dacombe, let it dwindle. The Achilles team, sensing victory, gained momentum and won by a convincing ten yards. It was quite a turnaround.

Ray Dodge was not the only American athlete on display. A whole team from Illinois AC had been invited to attend and one of their members was the great all-round track and field athlete, Harold Osborne, who had won gold medals in the high jump and decathlon at the 1924 Olympics. The American had arrogantly entered himself for nearly every event, only picking the ones he would compete in once he saw the schedule. He won a gold medal in the high jump and five silver medals. The press did not miss the chance to utilise their cartoonists in earnest. In the *Daily Express*, the bespectacled Osborne was sketched carrying a javelin in one hand and a vaulting pole in the other as he competed in the two events simultaneously. Cec was honoured to be depicted in a sketch in the *Daily Mail* with the tongue-in-cheek caption that 'C.R. Griffiths won the half mile as Mr Osborne was engaged elsewhere at the moment'.

Harry Barclay hardly treated the Illinois athletes with great respect. After Loren Murchison won the 100 and 220 yards sprints, his medals were temporarily withheld pending an investigation into his status as an amateur following information received that day. Barclay was still relentlessly pursuing his quest to eliminate the face of professionalism from the sport. The status and reputation of an athlete meant nothing to Barclay – he was once again hunting down an Olympic relay champion. Who knows whether Cec offered words of support to Murchison or what his inward feelings were at seeing his adversary go after another target. Murchison was subsequently awarded his medals after Barclay could find no evidence of wrongdoing. Later in the year, Murchison was struck down with meningitis and paralysed from the waist down. His AAA medals were among the last athletics prizes he won.

Of course, not every member of the AAA had it in for Cec and athletes like him. Committee member Charles Otway was a rare AAA ally. He generally felt let down by the unexpected failure of several notable athletes in the AAA Championship. He considered that, unlike the previous year's Olympic Games, many were not racing to the bitter end and gave up too easily when challenged. He admitted this in an article in the *Sporting Life and Sportsman*:

When all was over I was considering the whole meeting... there was just a little strain of disappointment over the home athlete's showing. And yet Rangeley and Rinkel ran finely, if they were beaten. Stallard, Griffiths and Gaby have never done much better. What was it? An American friend supplied the answer; "You've some great runners," he said, "but, my, you do have some quitters." That I think explained the situation.

Otway made clear that his criticisms did not apply to Cec, Stallard and Gaby, about whom he was full of praise, but he repeated his condemnation the following weekend when England lost the Fraternité Cup to France. Otway's frank views earned him an official reprimand from the AAA who regretted such a suggestion should have been made in the press by a member of the committee. No doubt they were also concerned that Otway was openly backing Cec, who he clearly thought was so much better than the rest. Indirectly, it was backing Cec that got him into trouble.

Cec had always enjoyed the annual England v France Fraternité Cup international, having gained a fine reputation across the Channel at the first three contests, so he was deeply frustrated by his exclusion from the event at Brighton on 25 July, the first following his ban. Attending as a spectator, he was delighted for Henry Stallard, who comfortably won an unexciting 800 metres in a time of 1:53.8, the second-fastest in Britain. Stallard was coming off the back of winning the 440 yards in the AAA Championship, where he became the only British athlete to win titles in the mile, half mile and quarter mile. In a reversal of the normal pattern, he had progressed to shorter events as he got older without any sacrifice in quality or ability. Stallard's ability to finish

880 yards in quick times meant that he was possibly the best British half miler of the moment, better even than Olympic Champion Douglas Lowe and AAA Champion Cec.

Critically, second and third places in the 800 metres were taken by French runners, as was also the case in the 400 metres. That earned them valuable points which contributed to them lifting the Fraternité Cup for the first time. Cec took some consolation from the widespread speculation that the overall result would have been different if he had competed and possibly a British record or even a world record in the 800 metres would have been achieved if he had been able to challenge Stallard.

On 8 August Cec returned to Fallowfield, scene of his spectacular 880 yards race the previous year, for the Sporting Chronicle Carnival. Cec ran again in the half mile handicap, giving away 40 yards to the other runners. It was not enough. The *Manchester Guardian* reported, 'Griffiths has a beautiful action and in the last quarter showed tremendous speed. He managed to overtake his opponents in the last ten yards.' He won with a time of 1:54.6 – identical to the time he had set at the same event the previous year, although in the interim Douglas Lowe had reduced the fastest time run by a British athlete to 1:53.4 at a meeting in Cambridge, Massachusetts. 'It was a great accomplishment, one we might have hoped for from a champion,' *Athletic News* trumpeted. The programme, with an unappealing full-page advert for tripe on the back cover, carried Cec's picture and a warm tribute to him, anticipating he would soon break the troublesome British record that was still held by Mel Sheppard. It listed the prizes for each event and Cec received a solid silver rose bowl valued at £7.7s., exactly the limit allowed by the AAA.

The following year's AAA Championship programme still did not credit Cec with equalling Cross and Stallard in their unofficial English record. Overlooking his performance once was understandable, but twice indicated a reluctance to do so.*

At the Crittall's Sports meeting on 29 August, the handicappers excelled themselves with their harsh treatment of the two AAA Champions they were fortunate to have as major attractions. The *Chelmsford Chronicle* described Fred Gaby winning his 120 yards hurdles heat in 'beautiful form' for which he was awarded a harsh handicap in the next round. He was made to owe an incredible 25 yards and not surprisingly 'unfortunately went down in the semi-final as it was felt his handicap mark was severe'. The *Chronicle* went on to report, 'Another great runner who was felt to have been handicapped to the very limit was C.R. Griffiths.' In the heats of the 880 yards, Cec was made to owe eight yards – to run 888 yards in total – but he still came through. He was allowed to start on scratch in the quarter-final but failed to progress any further. It was hardly surprising that he chose not to try his hardest in a competition where he felt the handicappers were applying the rules incorrectly and unfairly.

* The unofficial English record was only shown in the AAA programmes of 1925 and 1926. It probably created considerable confusion, being held by athletes from all UK nations and not being listed for all events. In 1928 (until 1960), official English native records were introduced for performances made in England or Wales by athletes born in England or Wales. For the half mile, Lowe's 1:53.8 set at Fallowfield on 16 July 1927 was recognised as the new record, overtaking the 1:54.6 previously achieved by Cross, Stallard and Cec (twice).

Critics in the press were concerned about Cec's potential dominance of handicap races. One unidentified article stated, 'in the event of Griffiths going the round of the provincial meetings he would sweep the boards.' Now that he was barred from international competition and the Olympics, there was a fear that Cec would travel the country, picking up prizes and preventing local talent from having a chance to shine. To combat this, handicappers were inconsistent and Cec was sometimes made to owe a distance, as at Crittall's Sports, making him run further than the rest of the field. It was the same situation that Albert Hill had faced a few years earlier; an eight yards penalty was levied on previous winners of open handicaps, but it should not have put an athlete back beyond the scratch mark.

This made a mockery of the races and meant that Cec had no ability to break records or better his times. Albert Hill had threatened to withdraw from meetings unless he was treated fairly, but Cec left it to the sporting press, notably the Welsh contingency, to argue his case. The *South Wales Echo*, in support of their champion, launched a stinging attack on the handicappers who they described as 'a law unto themselves' and appealed to the AAA Board of Control to take action.

Cec's response was often to vote with his feet and turn to meetings where he felt better treated. He was made to feel much more welcome at the Kennington Oval on 19 September, where he won the 880 yards scratch race and helped the Surrey AC team win the mile invitation relay. Cec was proud to compete on the ground which hosted the first Test cricket match in 1880 and was home to Surrey County

Cricket Club, whose members enjoyed strong links with and enthusiastically supported their local athletic club.

Away from the track, May was pregnant a second time, which necessitated another move of house. After seven years, Cec moved away from Maryland Park in Stratford to a bigger flat above a shop in Tanner Street, Barking, just in time for their second son to be born on 31 October. He was a second Cecil R. Griffiths in the family.

The young Cecil was always referred to as Rees, his middle name, which was also his mother's maiden name. He inherited traits from both his parents; he had his mother's colouring and fine features, his father's character and sporting prowess.

Rees was introduced to his wider family at Christmas, when Cec, May and their two sons journeyed to Agincourt House to spend the holiday with his mother. On 27 December, Rees was christened at St David's Church, in keeping with family tradition. Despite living in London and both their children being born there, Cec and May clearly considered their hearts and souls belonged at home with their families in Neath.

Good Old Griff – part of Cec's comprehensive autograph
collection with Halland Britton's tribute. Abrahams,
Barclay, Binks, Burghley, Butler and Lowe also feature.

14

THE GREATEST

HALF MILE

1926

At the start of the season Cec gave an in-depth interview at the shirt factory where he worked to a special correspondent for the *South Wales Echo*, who found him looking 'every inch an athlete, the very picture of radiant health and fitness'. The journalist explained that although Cec was engaged in business in London he still found plenty of time for training on the Great Eastern Railway ground at Stratford. Clearly

his employment by the Vowles family was mutually conve-
nient with plenty of time off for training and competition.

Cec revealed a lot of information about his past; that his
first race was at school when he was eleven, that he had won
a few junior handicaps before going to work for the railway
company, that he ran very little after then until he joined the
Army. He never thought of taking up athletics seriously until
after he left the Army in 1919 to join Surrey AC. It was an
unconventional route to athletics stardom, but one that was
far more familiar to the readers of the *South Wales Echo* than
the grassy quads of Oxford and Cambridge.

Yet Cec was not flattering about athletics in Wales:

> What they want in Wales is one or two good cinder tracks
> where the lads can train, and more encouragement for the
> youngsters. With the exception of Newport and a little in Car-
> diff, athletics seems to be dead in Wales.

Although critical of his small nation's efforts, he was
fiercely patriotic and gracious enough to pay tribute to 'good
men' including Abe Manning of Swansea and Cliff Price of
Newport Harriers, who he thought would have been one of
Wales' finest athletes if he had not lost a leg in the war.

He expressed his regret in not competing at the previous
year's Welsh Championship because of the clash with the
AAA Championship, explaining, 'I always look forward to
going down there', and hoped the meetings would not clash
in 1926.

The interviewer backed up Cec's patriotism by explaining, 'In presenting a cup for athletics at his old school in
Neath, Griffiths has set an excellent example to others who

wish to see Wales on a par with all countries in the athletic world.'

He discussed the reason for his ban and reminded the interviewer, 'I was, you remember, barred from representing Great Britain in the 1924 Olympic Games.' It clearly was still a topic of regret for him but he was philosophical, describing it as 'rather a set back at the time, but like most happenings such as this they are sent to try us'. His stiff upper lip in the face of adversity was just the type of English trait that would have impressed gentlemen of the AAA who banned him.

Yet Cec made his position on professionalism very clear:

Like many other branches of sport in South Wales, athletics have been marred by the introduction of professionalism.

He clearly found professionalism in athletics and sport to be distasteful. This explains one of the most puzzling questions about his athletics career – why didn't he turn professional and capitalise on his fame when he was branded with professionalism at his peak in 1923? Promoters of events were hungry to set up challenge races and organise record-breaking attempts because they knew large crowds would pay good money to share a slice of history in the making. Cec could have carried on running outside of the auspices of the AAA and earned a lot more money in doing so. Instead he chose to remain with one foot inside the AAA as a reinstated professional, never fully accepted.

When the interviewer returned to safer ground and asked Cec about his favourite races, Cec picked several but it was the Fallowfield races he talked about most. If the interview had been conducted at the end of the season rather than the start, there would have been some sublime additions to the list.

The 41st Essex Championship was held on 5 June at Crittalls Ground and Cec easily won the half mile, looking behind at the finish, for his fifth consecutive title. Jack Gillis also took his fifth title in the 440 yards, but absence through injury the previous year had spoiled his unbroken run. C.W. Cater also joined the exclusive five-title club, joining it by winning the two mile walk.

Douglas Lowe needed to lift his game to combat the up-coming threat posed by Henry Stallard. Midway between his Olympic 800 metres success in 1924 and his defence of the title in 1928, Lowe capitalised on every opportunity which came his way in 1926. At the annual Cambridge University AC v All England contest at Cambridge on 12 June, Lowe was in formidable form. He beat Cec in the half mile by six yards with 1:55.8, but it was not enough to secure overall honours for the Cantabs. At the evening's celebration dinner the visitors were in a buoyant mood. Cec's menu contained over sixty signatures and Halland Britton, who had tied for first place in the three miles race, summed up the team's attitude towards Cec when he wrote 'Good old Griff' beside his signature.

Lowe was running everywhere and anywhere. Rumour suggested that Cec was too, although it was not quite correct. A printing error in the *Gloucester Citizen* suggested that Cec and Stallard competed together at the United Hospital Athletic Championship at Crystal Palace in June 1926. Stallard won the half mile and mile races and ran the first leg in the winning medley relay team for St Bartholomew's Hospital, where he studied and worked. The newspaper also recorded C.R. Griffiths winning the 100 yards and 220 yards for Bart's. Cec was not a particularly strong sprinter (although he had won the 220 yards in the Welsh Championship in 1921) and this would be an unusual meeting for him to attend, but it was thought that Stallard had introduced Cec as a ringer to help Bart's to the hospital championship. The story wasn't quite so exciting. The sprints were won by T.R. (Thomas Reginald) Griffiths, who entered the medical college in 1924. Maybe if Cec had helped out, Guy's Hospital wouldn't have won the trophy.

Mistakes concerning athletes' names and initials were common; undoubtedly the casualties of copy being read over the telephone to meet a deadline or steal a march on the opposition. The written word was the only medium by which sports journalists could function. Reporting on sporting events was a lucrative industry with hacks vying to sell their scoops to newspapers which were packed with articles and statistics to satisfy an insatiable demand from the public for information. The more attractive their copy, the greater the likelihood was of an editor purchasing it in a very competitive market, and often they would carry multiple reports of the same event. Inevitably, there was a temptation to exaggerate and slide into hyperbole in order to add value to the finished product.

Stallard and Cec might not have appeared together at the United Hospital Championship, but in the middle of the decade they certainly competed against each other on the occasions when Stallard concentrated on the half mile. They also stood side by side in Gallaher's British Champions of 1923 cigarette cards. Cec and Stallard are numbers 72 and 73, celebrating their AAA Championship victories in the half mile and mile that year.

Cec was a smoker. There was nothing unusual about that, nearly every man in the country smoked, so it wouldn't have affected his running performances relative to his peers. His picture on the cigarette card made him a household name; his performance in the 1926 AAA Championship made it unlikely that anybody would forget it anytime soon.

On 3 July, Cec took part in arguably his greatest ever race. Joe Binks had confidently predicted that Douglas Lowe, the Olympic champion, would be pressed into making a new world record for the half mile by Cec, but none of them counted on a German spoiling the party. As usual, the AAA had sent invitations abroad so the national championship was an international affair. For the first time since before the war, the AAA had invited a strong contingent of Germans, including their greatest middle-distance runner, Dr Otto Peltzer.

The crowd of 20,000 had been warmed up by six heats of 100 yards sprints, five of which were won by Germans – this was a strong cohort from the continent. Pre-race publicity had seized on Binks' prediction and billed the 880 yards as 'record breaking', so as the entrants lined up, with the high jump and hammer competitions already in progress, there was a charged atmosphere of great expectation. Henry Stallard was absent, reportedly giving blood to save the life of a patient at St Bartholomew's, but Peltzer was ready to test himself against Lowe and Cec.

Lowe took the lead from the gun with Peltzer third and Cec trailing in last place, clearly happy to keep an eye on proceedings. Lowe covered the first lap in 54.6, by which time Peltzer had moved up to second and Cec had come through the rest of the field to third, pushing them both hard. Peltzer, shadowed by Cec, began to speed up and put pressure on with 300 yards to go. Lowe held them off and increased his lead by a few strides. His triumph looked to be a formality, but along the final straight, as the three outstanding athletes thundered towards the line, Peltzer made an electrifying sprint to steal the victory from Lowe.

It had clearly been a very fast race. The crowd hushed in anticipation of the winning time. Suddenly they broke into ecstasy when they heard the announcement. Peltzer's 1:51.6 had beaten Ted Meredith's world record of 1:52.2, as had Lowe in an estimated time of 1:52.0. Cec's estimated time of 1:53.1 was within the existing British record, but that had also fallen to the German. Peltzer's time also took the 800 metres world record, knocking 0.3 seconds off that particular figure.

There was no question of there being any errors on the part of the timekeepers. The official in charge was using the best watches available which measured to one-hundredth of a second and cost a substantial £190. Peltzer was a new world record holder. After the furore of the sensational victory had subsided, in accordance with the rules required to establish a world record, the track was measured and found to be one foot too long. Peltzer had actually run further than he needed to, and still broke the world record.

Lowe and Cec had run the two fastest ever half miles (and two feet) by British athletes. Although their times were unofficial and their second and third placed finishes do not count towards the lists of all-time best British performances, Cec's time was still a personal best and the best performance in the 880 yards by a Welsh athlete.[*] No wonder that the race was described in *Athletic News* as 'the most wonderful race in the history of athletics' and 'the greatest half mile ever'.

Peltzer also ran in the quarter mile, the last race of the day, and took part in another spectacular finish. This time, in a fast and close contest, it was John Rinkel of Cambridge University AC who tested Peltzer right to the line; the Englishman took the win by a foot. The exertion and emotion of the day had exhausted Peltzer and he fainted in the dressing room, but he soon recovered to receive his trophies at a lively prize-giving ceremony.

Peltzer's supreme talent was confirmed when, two months later, he took the 1,500 metres world record at a special challenge meeting in Berlin, beating former record holder Paavo Nurmi in the process. He turned down the unimaginable sum of $250,000 to tour the USA, saying, 'A sportsman does not need financial compensation, since the act carries its own reward.' Peltzer was driven instead by a desire to represent a rehabilitated Germany at the 1928 Olympic Games, the first German representation in the Olympics for sixteen years.

---

[*] It was equalled by Jim Alford in 1938 but not beaten until 1959 by Tony Harris of Mitcham AC.

On 10 July, a week after the landmark race with Peltzer and Lowe, Cec was at Hampden Park in Glasgow for the annual Triangular International Contest. Cec narrowly beat Scotland's William Seagrove, a Cambridge Blue, in a time of 1:57.2, equalling Lowe's record for the Triangular Internationals. The sprint finish was very necessary as Seagrove had clung on to Cec right round the track. English athletes dominated and at the official dinner, held at the Bank Restaurant in Glasgow, Cec passed around the official menu for all to sign after their meal of assorted meats and chips.

Charles Otway in *Athletic News* described Cec as 'a runner who always does his best in relays if he has a big task'. It is hard to disagree. Although a recognised 880 yards specialist, there is no doubt Cec saved many of his best performances for relays. He proved that at Stamford Bridge in the Inter-County Championship on 17 July where he ran his fastest ever 440 yards in the 4x440 yards relay. Running the anchor leg for the Essex team, he was matched against Middlesex's John Rinkel, who could even boast of beating Peltzer. When Cec's best friend, Jack Gillis, handed him the baton, Rinkel had a fifteen-yard advantage and was 'going like a steam train'. In a super display of raw pace, Cec closed the gap to within a yard, but the effort was too much to sustain and he dropped back to finish second, three yards behind. To have closed the gap to the AAA Champion by a reported twelve yards was astonishing.

Rinkel's winning leg was 49.8, but Cec's unofficial time was 48.2. If confirmed, it would have broken the British record and was 1.6 seconds faster than his personal best. Being a relay and finishing second, the time did not qualify for record status, but Charles Otway opined, 'We realised that Griffiths had run the race of his life... which shows what relay racing may bring out of a man.'

The top performances continued in a golden July for middle-distance running. On the 25th of the month, in the Fraternité Cup meeting in Paris, Douglas Lowe narrowly failed to take Peltzer's newly-set 800 metres world record. Lowe ran a lone race against a poor quality field, prompting the press to speculate once again whether the record would have been taken if Cec had been allowed to compete. Cec's ban made that impossible.

There must have been rumours that Cec was considering retiring at the end of 1926 if a report in the *Cambridge Daily News* was to be believed. He had entered the half mile handicap at the popular annual meeting held on the testing track at Chivers Sports Ground which surrounded a sloping football pitch in Histon, near Cambridge. The event, involving both athletics and cycling, was advertised as 'The Famous Histon Sports For British And National Champions'. Cec, obviously a big draw, received top billing from the club's press officer (who clearly enjoyed using capital letters to emphasise his sentiments):

> Cecil Griffiths (Surrey AC). The World's Most Marvellous Half-Mile Flat Handicap Runner ever yet known; and without a doubt the most Prolific Championship Winner for a Decade. He holds the wonderful record of winning the Histon Half-Mile Flat Handicap Three Years in Succession off the Scratch Mark, and is out to win this race again for the fourth year before retiring.

By all accounts the half mile was a great race, exemplifying Cec's skill in handicaps. With a field of 28 to negotiate his way through on a short track with a steady incline on the home straight, his task was literally uphill. The crowd spurred him on as he ran an exceptional last lap, putting on a final spurt up the slope to win by two yards with a meritorious time of 1:59.0.

Charles Otway was absolutely correct in his assessment of Cec as being strongest in relays, but he could just as easily have extended his words of praise to cover his efforts in handicaps. Cec certainly enjoyed the thrill of the chase.

Part of the family – Cec with Nanny Woodroffe and
a Surrey AC teammate, thought to be Edward Wheller.

15

A Neath
World's Record
1927-1929

Cec won his sixth consecutive title at the Essex Championships at Southend on 21 May 1927 in a race the *Chelmsford Chronicle* described as the 'Tit Bit of the meeting won by the clever half mile athlete'. The other men with five titles who could have emulated his feat, C.W. Cater and Jack Gillis, both failed.

Nevertheless, there were a few chinks appearing in his armour. Exactly a week later, Cec secured a sixth consecutive placing in the top three at the Kinnaird Trophy meeting at Stamford Bridge; but it was the first time he hadn't won either the 440 yards or the 880 yards since 1922. The *South Wales Echo* had a long memory when they reported that the 'Olympic champion' ran a great race in the 880 yards, narrowly losing in a fast time to Henry Stallard. They were delighted for their local hero and ended with a fine tribute:

> He has put up some exceptionally fast times for the half-mile, and is a popular competitor at all the big meetings in England and Scotland. Neath should be proud of him.

Then, at the Welsh Championship held on Penarth Recreation Ground on 6 June, Cec's fourth double title narrowly eluded him. He won the 880 yards in a slow time to take his tenth and last Welsh title, but only came second in the 440 yards. It was his last appearance in the Welsh Championship.

Was Cec's pace beginning to fail, or was he just out of form? Perhaps the answer was that he was under the weather. On 11 June, Cec was scheduled to face Lowe in the half mile of the annual Cambridge University AC v AAA Test at Fenner's. Cec was unwell and withdrew, to be replaced by mile specialist Cyril Ellis. Ellis found his best form in the shorter distance and surprisingly beat Lowe, passing him on the back straight.

Cec was rested and recovered by the time the AAA Championship came round on 2 July, although he was not good enough to reclaim his 880 yards title that had been lost to Peltzer in the amazing 1926 race. This time, Cec was second behind Douglas Lowe, whose winning time was 1:54.6. Lowe must have been glad not to have been pressed too hard by Cec as he had to run in the final of the 440 yards two hours later, winning a second title, and was then part of the 4x440 yards Achilles relay team which beat a team from Surrey AC with Cec on the anchor leg. Lowe was the second British track athlete, after Cec, to have previously won an Olympic gold medal before picking up his first AAA title. Winning three AAA titles in one day was the icing on the cake.

At the end of the month, Cec was the star attraction at a sports festival organised jointly by Neath RFC and the local YMCA. No doubt Cec would have wanted a big crowd to cheer him round his home track, but the expected multitude didn't materialise so only a few witnessed an apparent miracle in the half mile handicap. Cec's raw speed was far in excess of his competitors and he won the demonstration race with ease, but Cec was as dumbfounded as the timekeepers when they checked their watches – he had broken Peltzer's world record by 0.4 seconds. However, after some hasty measurements it was discovered the track was on the short side. Still, that didn't stop the *South Wales Echo* from headlining its report, 'A Neath World's Record? A Trap For Timekeepers.'

Then, for the second weekend in a row, Cec was involved in something of a disastrous record race. At Ibrox Park in Glasgow on 6 August, Cec competed in a 600 yards invitation handicap at the annual Rangers Sports. The specially-framed race had been set up in order for Douglas Lowe to attempt an assault on the long-standing 1906 British record, which he had already beaten in an unrecognised run the previous year. He was eager to break the record for real, and Cec (wrongly described as a Birchfield Harrier) found himself in the unusual situation of making up the numbers and working as a pacemaker for Lowe from an eight-yard handicap. It was a disaster. Lowe only came fourth, three seconds outside his target, while Cec was third.

On 13 August, the usually-strong Essex relay teams only finished second in both 4x440 and 4x880 yards events at the Inter-Counties meeting, despite being given a helping hand by the Kent team in the 440 yards race. As the Kent runner came to finish the third leg, he found he had nobody to hand the baton over to. Cec was the only one who ran in both relays, taking the anchor leg in each, just failing to overtake the winner on both occasions. *Sporting Life* thought the blame might lie at the feet of Cec, suggesting underneath the caption 'Griffiths Stale?' that 'the little Welshman is not quite his old self, or he might have given Essex two victories'. The *Daily Express* held a different opinion, describing his two close relay battles with William Craner in the quarter mile and Wilfred Tatham in the half mile as 'worth going a long way to see'.

Relays had been a vital element in Cec's success over his career, and in recent years his all-important first leg of 880 yards in the mile medley relay had set up many victories for Surrey AC and Essex. However, in 1927 the AAA dabbled with the formats of the relays, introducing 4x100 and 4x440 yards races. It heralded the demise of the mile medley relay, one of Cec's favoured events.

Immediately below the article in the *Sporting Life* that suggested Cec was stale, a report described a Welsh £140 Sprint, held on the same day as the Inter-Counties Championship. It was a sprint handicap race at the Taff Vale Park, Pontypridd; a track Cec was familiar with, but clearly a race for professionals. It was far removed from the auspices of the AAA and exactly the kind of event that their rules were designed to prevent elite athletes from taking part in. However, it made Cec's misdemeanour of £3 prizes in 1917 pale into insignificance, showing them up as the triviality they were.

On 20 August, Cec put the frustrating performances of the previous three weeks behind him. He was back on form, winning the mile open relay at the Reading Mortimer Sports Club. His margin of victory was so great that there was no other runner in sight as he broke the tape.

Suggesting that Cec was stale might have been overdoing it, but as the 1928 season dawned, Cec was in his late-twenties and recognised that he was coming into the twilight of his athletics career. Nevertheless, he started the year with his longest competitive run, in the London to Brighton relay race on 14 April, as one of the ten members of the Surrey AC team. Cec ran the second leg from Clapham Common to Mitcham, a distance of 4 miles 1056 yards, in 25 minutes 20 seconds.

Cec's last Kinnaird Trophy race was on 26 May, and he finished in third place in the half mile. That was followed by a successful defence of his 880 yards title at the Essex Championship on 9 June at the Garrison Cricket Ground, Colchester. Conditions were not easy; it was blowing a severe gale, but the wind was Cec's toughest opponent: the quality of the competition was diluted as the championship clashed with the AAA v Cantabs at Fenner's in Cambridge. Still, Cec could only beat those runners who were in the same race, and he safely did that for a seventh successive title.

Cec did not enter the Welsh Championship held at Newport Athletic Ground on 16 June for reasons unknown, but it was unlikely to be illness. The following weekend, Cec was in fine form to win the last of his three AAA Southern Counties titles on the Oxford University track, and three days later he competed in Scotland.

The Tramway Meeting held at Helenvale Park was a three-way team competition between Scotland, Surrey AC and Birchfield Harriers AC. The *Glasgow Evening Times* reported that the 'English cracks do well' and were pleased that it was 'the old Griffiths' on display. Cec took the first leg of 880 yards in the mile medley relay against Scottish champion Donald MacLean and Cyril Ellis of Birchfield Harriers. In a trademark race which had the crowd of 7,000 on their feet, Cec kept within striking distance of the other two and surged past them to hand over first to Jack Gillis. Unfortunately the rest of the Surrey men couldn't maintain it and the Birchfield team won the race. In a fast, closely-fought individual 600 yards race, Cec was a disappointing fourth, but only four yards behind the winner. The newspaper offered a warm tribute despite his two defeats:

> Griffiths was nearer to the Griffiths of old than he has been this season, and once again he gave the Glasgow public, as he has often done in the past, a glimpse of real good running.

Their words may have been kind but their cartoon of Cec, reflecting his advancing years, did him no favours. Cec did not want to be a shadow of his old self, trading on his reputation as an Olympian of days gone by, he wanted to remain a front-runner.

The mind may have been willing, but the body may not have been able. At the 1928 AAA Championship on 7 July, Cec failed to finish in the top three of an individual event for the first time in ten years. Watched by 40,000 people, including five-year-old John in the stand, he came fourth in the half mile. To be fair to Cec, the circumstances of the race went against him. A slow first lap saw the runners bunched up as they heard the bell. Douglas Lowe led the charge away from the pack on the back straight pursued by Hermann Engelhard, but Cec was not able to follow – he was spiked in the melee of legs and left limping over the line. Cec could have been the victim of a professional foul, but more likely it was an accident. Considering his years running in close proximity to others, Cec was probably lucky that it only happened once.

Cec retained a news vendor's billboard with a hazy picture of the finish of the race. Lowe won courtesy of a final burst, Engelhard was a close second. Cec can clearly be seen grimacing back in fourth place. It was a shock for John to see his father bloodily injured, forcing him to spend a couple of weeks on crutches and effectively ending his season.*

Other athletes were beginning to reach their peak in time for the 1928 Olympic Games in Amsterdam and the *Sporting Life* accurately forecast that the AAA Championship would be 'practically an Olympiad on a minor scale'. British records were taken by German Ernst Paulus in the discus and Stan Lay, the New Zealander, in the javelin. The championship doubled up as the 1928 Olympic trials. Although Cec was allowed to take part, there was never any chance or hope of him being included in the British team which was selected immediately after the meeting. If he had been eligible for selection, his injury would have been a disaster. Instead, it was a minor inconvenience.

Lowe was free to defend his Olympic 800 metres title on 31 July. His second gold medal came in a time of 1:51.8, an Olympic record and the best time by a British athlete. It sealed Lowe's place in athletics history.

Cec's duels with Lowe in the latter part of the decade were an echo of those he had with Edgar Mountain a few years earlier. Pure results would suggest Lowe was the best half mile runner, and Cec would probably have agreed. Yet without the international ban, Cec would have competed, like Lowe, more widely throughout the world and against the best opposition. Cec could certainly beat Lowe on any given day – the AAA Championship in 1923 and Kinnaird Trophy in 1924 were proof enough of that. Who knows

---

* It was a short term setback for Cec but for John, only five, it was traumatic and left a lasting impression on him. It was one of the first things he told me about his father when we first met.

what heights he may have reached by being tested on the international stage?

The first evidence of Cec attempting to race after his injury was at Crittalls Sports Ground on 31 August, some three weeks after the Olympic closing ceremony, where he was entered to start on scratch in the half mile handicap. The cinder track had been rendered unsafe by the heat wave earlier in the summer, making it necessary to cancel the cycle races – no cyclist wanted to crash on the soft, slippery ground. It was decided to proceed with the track events, but it was a risk not worth taking for Cec, especially considering that the handicappers, as was often the case, had levied a penalty beyond scratch. He would have to aggressively overtake the entire field of competitors on unstable ground amidst flying spikes, and memories of his mishap at Stamford Bridge were fresh in his mind. It was prudent to withdraw.

Cec simply did not have anything to prove. After all, he had raced in, and won, many great contests. Just in case anybody needed convincing, Joe Binks dedicated a detailed and glorious tribute to Cec in the *News of the World*. Like the man it profiled, it was simple and to the point: 'Greatest Half-Mile Races Of C.R. Griffiths.'

*

On 13 January 1929, John's sixth birthday, a man turned up at the Griffiths' flat in Barking with a large box under his arm. He watched the excited lad rip open his present to reveal an expensive Hornby train set, the first of their new electrical products, which would have cost a considerable amount of money. He helped John set up the track and wire it up to the mains then happily spent the whole evening sitting on the floor beside him playing with it.*

The visitor was David Cecil, better known as Lord Burghley, the aristocratic hurdler who became the sixth Marquess of Exeter when his father died in 1956. Burghley was to marry for the first time later in the year and would have five children with his two wives, but on that winter day in 1929 it was a novel and obviously enjoyable experience for him to play at length with a child.

Cec clearly had the confidence and grace to be comfortable within any class of society, having matured from the young man who felt overawed by the Surrey AC dinner in 1921. Both Cec and May were very upset by the way Cec had been treated by the gentlemen of the AAA who ran his sport. Burghley was from that ruling class; he was titled, an Achilles man who enjoyed advantages Cec would never experience. Their lives were worlds apart; one had a father brought up in a London workhouse; the other had a father who sat in the House of Lords. Yet despite the chasm between them, Burghley held his Welsh mentor, five years his senior, in high esteem. To Cec, a friend was a friend, regardless.

---

* John told me about this in one of our early conversations. Like the spiking of his father, it had imprinted itself on his young mind. The only other toy he remembered was a Meccano construction set which was added to every Christmas and birthday, so the train set was something special. I was sceptical regarding the level of detail in which John described the visit and the present: a Hornby Bassett-Lowke locomotive with three carriages in the brown and cream livery of the Great Western Railway, powered by the new six-volt DC operating system. I couldn't believe he was able to remember so much, but an internet search soon located the exact model he described. Despite his youth at the time and his failing memory in old age, John still cherishes that encounter with the nobleman who sparked his lifelong passion for steam trains.

When Cec first came across Burghley, he was a student at
Magdalene College, Cambridge who won the AAA Championship 440 yards hurdles race, breaking the British record
twice in the process. The aristocratic hurdler perfected his
technique in training by placing matchboxes on the hurdles
and removing them with pin-point accuracy with his lead
foot as it narrowly cleared the woodwork.

Cec took an increasing interest in Burghley's career and
raised a glass in celebration every time he achieved a new
record. He became the first man to sprint the quarter mile
around the Great Court at Trinity College, Cambridge within the 43 seconds it took the college clock to toll 12 o'clock.
In 1927 Burghley defended his 440 yards hurdles AAA title,
accomplishing his only world record at the same time, but
it was short-lived. His time of 54.2 was beaten by Johnny
Gibson a few hours later in Nebraska. The following year,
he reached the pinnacle of his career, winning one of the
three gold medals won by Great Britain at the 1928 Olympic Games.

Nor was Cec's friendship with Burghley a one-off. During
1923, Cec had struck up a close friendship with Bill Nevill, President of Surrey AC and fourth son of the Marquess
of Abergavenny. In one moving letter, Nevill apologised for
some kind of disagreement or misunderstanding between
them. He told Cec how he valued their friendship, addressing him as his best friend, and said that he was thankful that
his presidency of Surrey AC had brought them together. He
expressed his delight that Cec had won one of his prizes
to remember him by when he had 'gone west', presumably

the relay cup in his name which he presented at the annual dinner.*

Lord Nevill was born in 1860, the same year as Cec's father. Since the age of eight, Cec had not experienced the love or support of a paternal figure – Bill Nevill would have filled that role for him during his years as an athlete in London. For the distinguished lord, Cec's friendship was something that his privilege and wealth could not provide, especially considering that he had no children of his own.

At the Surrey AC dinner on 30 January 1929, presided over by his friend Lord Nevill, Cec passed around his menu, as normal, for all to sign. Harry Barclay responded to the Visitors' Toast and Cec proposed the Toast to the Club. The menu from this function was the last one which Cec customised in his usual manner. It did not contain Barclay's signature. Those that he did collect on menus from the many functions he attended throughout his career, in addition to the ones he amassed at the 1920 Olympic Games, probably represents the most comprehensive collection of athletes' autographs from the 1920s.

In February 1929, Cec stood for election to the AAA Southern Committee. It was a surprising move having been treated so harshly by the AAA in the run up to the 1924 Olympics. Cec was contemplating retirement from active athletics and perhaps intended to influence the administration from within, but it was a foregone conclusion that his

---

* 'Bill' had first written to Cec in 1923, revealing that he travelled widely to watch Cec and sent him regular press cuttings of his races. The clue to his identity was the discovery of his signature on a series of wall calendars, all bearing the same picture of Eridge Castle in Tunbridge Wells, the seat of the Marquess of Abergavenny. 'Bill' was actually Lord William Nevill.

intention to infiltrate the body which had so influenced his destiny would fail. As a reinstated professional with a working-class background and lack of formal education, he was not the kind of person the AAA was looking for. Although he received 92 votes, he needed double that to dislodge any of the Achilles brethren from their lofty perches. Harold Abrahams was newly elected with 177 votes, his fellow Cambridge alumnus Douglas Lowe re-elected with 211.

A.B. George must have picked up on the hints that 1929 would be Cec's last year of competition at the top echelon of the sport. Writing a technical article on the ideal running action in *All Sports Weekly*, he cited Cec's style as an example to young athletes and reminisced how Cec had been pointed out to him as a champion-in-waiting back in 1918. He ended with the words, 'It is good to reflect that we have experienced athletes like Griffiths in our clubs, as their example and advice plays an important part in the development of young runners.' It was the last time George would write about Cec.

Other writers who knew Cec, some of them his athletics compatriots, chose not to recognise his style or pay him the compliments he deserved. Douglas Lowe and his Achilles teammate, New Zealander Arthur Porritt, jointly published a book titled *Athletics* in 1929. Its historical, technical and medical content were extremely detailed and introduced some advanced theories concerning the well-being of athletes, most interestingly the effects of alcohol and tobacco on the body. The passage on holding the baton covered several pages and demonstrated to the uninitiated that it was certainly far from simple.

The authors attempted to ascribe the success of different classes of athletes to their physical stature, illustrating the theory where possible with examples, such as the 440 yards: 'Butler is a true quarter miler of tremendous build and strength, 6 feet and 3 inches, long striding and of great build and lung capacity.'

Lowe was too modest to associate himself with the half mile, so in his description of such specialist athletes he mentioned Henry Stallard and 1908 Olympic gold medallist Mel Sheppard:

> The middle-distance runner is almost invariably spare and slim, of medium height, long in the leg, with a springy carriage, quite deep chested, and possessed of great powers of endurance and a real share of nervous energy. The muscular development is less pronounced than in the case of the sprinter, length taking the place of thickness; and although the quarter miler may be a middle or even a heavyweight, the true middle-distance runner is light in weight, with length of stride as compensation.

Cec perfectly fitted Lowe's description, so it was a shame for him to ignore his Welsh rival. Lowe also missed his opportunity to pay him due respect when describing the importance of style in the book. He wrote, 'good style has been said to induce economy of effort.' Cec's long, elegant stride combined with his classic piston arm method made him one of the most stylish runners of his generation, and he must have been in Lowe's thoughts when he put pen to paper.

Cec did not seem to have the warm friendship with Lowe that he had with other Achilles men like Lord Burghley. In the 1926 AAA Championship race where Peltzer broke the world record, Cec and Lowe ran the two fastest half miles by British athletes. They had raced against each other many times and both shared the rare accolade of winning an Olympic gold medal before becoming a British Champion, so Lowe must have appreciated Cec's fine qualities. However, there is no record of either man particularly praising the other and they rarely raced against each other in non-championship meetings. Perhaps Cec and Lowe smply did not get on.

Cec's final season was a relatively low key affair. He did not enter the Welsh or AAA Championships, nor the Kinnaird Trophy, but he continued to compete in other events. In the Essex Championship at Leyton on 20 July he won his eighth and final title, but because of severe heat and other attractions in the area, only a small crowd witnessed the unparalleled feat. The *Chelmsford Chronicle* described the meeting as one of the best in recent years and that 'Griffiths appears to be unbeatable'. They were correct. Essex county athletes were never given another chance to test him on the track.

On 29 August 1929, Cec ran in the most significant race of his final season and one which summed up his entire career. He was chosen to captain a mixed team of track and field athletes in a match between Wales and Achilles to be held in Swansea as part of their annual sports and gala. One last time, the working-class lad from South Wales had the chance to take on the gentlemen of Oxford and Cambridge Universities.

The event was marred by the Welsh weather which caused a tennis exhibition on the green to be abandoned along with the boxing and dancing contests. Impervious to the inclement conditions, the hardy Welsh team narrowly won the athletics by triumphing in five of the nine events. One of those victories belonged to Cec in the 880 yards. Achilles' E.H. Fryer was second, he had been in the winning 4x440 yards relay team at the 1929 AAA Championship. C.E.D. Goodhart, also of Achilles, was third.

At the prize presentation, smartly dressed in his suit with his hair slicked down, Cec was dwarfed by the massive Swansea Town Shield awarded to his winning team. He posed proudly with it for the photographers and claimed to not recognise himself when the photograph appeared in the newspapers because he was not wearing vest and shorts.

Dressing in a suit was something that Cec was going to have to get used to. After a decade of competing at the highest level, he decided to hang up his spikes at the end of the season and concentrate on the next phase of life with his family.

No more athletics vests – a smart Cec, now retired from
running

16

IT'S ONLY THE GOLD THAT MATTERS
1930-1938

As Cec retired, the Roaring Twenties were coming to an end. The economy had recovered after the First World War. Standards of living were improving. People could go into shops and purchase a new car, telephones or radio on credit – buy now, pay later. Surely the golden age was going to carry on into the next decade.

Sarah, Cec's mother, had put Agincourt House up for sale as it was too much for her to maintain in old age and had become very run down. Cec, Ben and Eva agreed to have her living with each of them in turn for four months a year. This put Cec and his family under a degree of pressure each time she came – his small Barking flat was not ideal – so he looked for a larger home in the area. He found the ideal property in Tomswood Hill, Barkingside. The rent was much higher and it would involve cycling sixteen miles a day to and from work, but that didn't seem to cause too much of a problem. His job was secure, he was no longer spending money travelling to athletics meetings and they would all benefit from the larger house and garden. He signed on the dotted line and they moved in the autumn of 1929. The timing couldn't have been worse.

Just as Cec and May were settling into a hard working but comfortable family routine, the most sudden and dramatic change ever known in the world's economy began. On 29 October 1929, known as Black Tuesday, stock markets throughout the world collapsed following a fall in US share prices. The effect of the Wall Street Crash was rapid and drastic. Manufacturing and trade, notably in heavy industries such as shipbuilding, saw a decline of as much as 90% in some areas. Unemployment in the UK bit hard, rising from 1 million to 2.5 million in 1930, with an inevitable drop in demand for most goods. As the new decade dawned, the rich lost vast fortunes and the workers struggled to survive, often suffering terrible hardship in the process.

The Vowles' shirt factory was not exempt from the economic downturn. By May 1931 it was suffering severe cash flow difficulties and the management found the company unable to pay its employees or suppliers. Cec's wages became spasmodic or paid in kind with shirts. When Cec's mother arrived for her stay in London, she was horrified to discover the family in such a plight. She wrote to Eva, who was also struggling to make ends meet in Porthcawl, swearing her to secrecy regarding the contents of the letter in case Cec found out.

Sarah reported that 'things are rotten indeed at the factory' and Cec, on half pay, was 'dull in the head' with worry. In order to feed the boys he was going permanently hungry and trying to sell shirts to buy food. She criticised Cec for moving to their 'damned expensive old house' (possibly not realising that he had acquired it specifically to house her visits) which at 25 shillings a month was double the rent of their old home and so far from 'the smoke' that he spent much more time cycling to work. She only had ten shillings herself and sent it to Eva, who appeared to be in an even more desperate state, suggesting that they sell some of the furniture and use her room for a lodger as she could sleep in the front room when she came to stay. Sarah offered some comfort by explaining that her brother George was painting Agincourt House with the intention of selling it, so she would be able to help out her children.

On 31 July 1931, six weeks after her previous letter to Eva, Sarah wrote again with the news that after three nearly payless months, Cec had lost his job that day with the closure of the factory. She repeated her complaints about the expensive house, which she now hated, and wondered how they were going to cope with poverty. The letter was short and full of anguish, an indication of the stress she was under worrying about her children, ending pessimistically, 'I can't say what the devil his family to do, not I.' She made no mention of Cec's state of mind, but it doesn't take much to imagine how he felt.

Getting another job during the Great Depression wasn't a simple solution. Countless others were in a similar situation – Jack Gillis revealed that his brother had been out of work for twelve months. The outlook was bleak. With no social security safety net for help and subsistence in times of need, having received no wages for months and without savings, their crisis was immediate and Cec had few options.

Cec faced a desperate choice. He was well aware that he had one source of money stored in the house. One evening, he laid out all of his medals and trophies on the kitchen table. John helped his father open the little medal boxes and cabinets, but he didn't understand the reason why his father wanted them all taken out. Several of the medals contained gold and there were dozens of silver cups and bowls worth several pounds. If the £7.7s. rose bowl he won at Fallowfield in 1925 was anything to go by, he had a good sum of money on the table. The average salary in 1931 was less than £200, so his trophies and medals offered a potential survival fund and invaluable security while he sought another job.

May was initially horrified but Cec was a pragmatist. To him they were just trinkets and his family's well-being was paramount. John and Rees enjoyed handling the captivating medals, some very shiny, others adorned in brightly coloured enamel, as their father told them the story of the race behind each one. Cec would miss showing them off to his boys, but they had heard it all before and their interests were expanding into many new areas.

Although Cec probably knew Agincourt House was going to be sold, he needed money immediately. Eva was also struggling and, although Ben was better off than his siblings, his clothes shop in Neath was also feeling the bite of the depression. Cec's pride would never have allowed him to contemplate asking his brother for a loan. Not long afterwards, Ben was forced to sell the business and moved to London to work for Austin Reed.

The next day, with no options left open to him, Cec went to a pawnbroker on the Kilburn High Road to present a selection of his trophy collection to the proprietor. He watched as the pawnbroker painstakingly and silently examined and weighed each item. Cec, frustrated by his lack of curiosity, tried to explain the significance of the 1923 and 1925 AAA Championship 15 carat gold medals in an effort to secure the best possible offer. The response he received from the disinterested businessman shocked him. Without a flicker of emotion, he said, 'Sir, it's only the gold that matters.'

Cec couldn't have chosen a worse time to sell gold. The price was at its lowest for a century. Within three years it would bounce back to double what it was at the time Cec sold his collection. 15 carat gold is 62.5% pure, so one of the championship medals weighing 33 grams, based on the average global gold price of $17 per ounce in 1931, would have raised Cec less than £5.

The only enthusiasm the old man mustered was when Cec showed him his Olympic gold medal and was asked where he got it from. The question would have brought back memories of heady days in August 1920 when Cec made his only Olympic appearance, so early in his career. He would have remembered carrying it in his pocket at the 1921 Surrey AC annual dinner, leading to Jack Gillis' reassuring comment that only two people in the room had a gold medal with them, the start of a warm, lifelong friendship.

Only one Welsh track or field athlete had won an Olympic gold medal before Cec and Jack Ainsworth-Davies ran into the history books, so the item which caught the eye of the pawnbroker was one of only three of its kind in existence. Cec considered himself lucky to have been allowed to keep it, fearing the IOC would strip him of his title and the medal for violating the rules of amateurism. They had done exactly that with the American Jim Thorpe who had won both the pentathlon and decathlon at Stockholm in 1912 and was subsequently discovered to have competed in baseball as a semi-professional.* The IOC had refrained from such draconian action in Cec's case, possibly showing a degree of sympathy for the young Welsh athlete, but at the same time being bound by its own rules.

A deal was struck. Cec returned home with enough cash to keep the family going but without a permanent means of income. He would have been acutely aware it was only a stopgap solution.

It is not known in what order he sold his medals and trophies or how many at a time, but John believes his father delved into the collection several times to raise some money. The family mood was very low for a long time. Cec cycled

* In 1982, thirty years after Thorpe's death, the medals were restored by the IOC and replicas of them were given to his family.

for miles each week to search for work, returning home physically and mentally exhausted, chasing every hint of a job and despairing at his constant failure. He would often get in late, feeling depressed. If they were still up, John and Rees would be kept at bay while he ate the meal which was waiting for him. Invariably his mood would not lift. The days merged into one long, unhappy period.

Not a single silver trophy of the considerable quantity he won is now known to exist. Only a few medals of low intrinsic value were retained. Cec hid the remaining ones away, probably because he couldn't bear to be reminded of the loss of objects so dear to him. The subject of their sale became taboo for the rest of his life, but those few items that remained were handed down to his family; two medals he won against Gaston Féry in 1921, the relay medal he won a few days before he was married and the 1924 bronze tablet from Stockholm. They are priceless to his descendants. More important than their physical presence is the knowledge of the circumstances surrounding their existence. They are tokens of the emotions associated with a great personal adventure.

Cec's mother was dismayed at the sale of the items which represented Cec's place in history. Her brother George had always been proud of the trophies he won playing rugby for Neath, especially as he got older when those halcyon days were a distant memory. She had been through some tough times, especially after her husband died, and did not have many tangible and meaningful reminders of her life. The knowledge that her children and grandchildren were staring at the same spectre of poverty that she knew only too well would have been a crushing blow for her aspirations of a happy and content old age. Within a month of writing her last letter to Eva, Sarah suffered a heart attack and died. Her body was taken to Paddington by a horse-drawn hearse, then on to Neath by train where she was buried at Llantwit cemetery, finally reunited with her husband Benjamin.

While dealing with her death, Cec discovered his mother's long-carried secret – she was nearly a year older than Benjamin, yet all through their married life she had maintained she was a year younger than him. Presumably to avoid the social stigma of, at the age of nearly 33, having married a younger man than herself, she had hidden her true age.

Following Sarah's death, Agincourt House was sold and the proceeds split between her children, something of a blessing for all three. Cec was out of work for a year before he obtained employment in 1932 with the London Co-operative Society (LCS), at their coal depot office in Edgware. It was a secure job and the salvation it offered, at a time when three million people were desperate for work, cannot be understated. He had applied for many posts but his lack of education and qualifications repeatedly conspired against him. Ultimately, his character won through. His sharp, organised mind was recognised by his new employer as ideal for the responsible duty of organising the procurement and distribution of thousands of tons of coal within the organisation.

With a steady job to rely on, did Cec look back and regret selling his medals the previous year? In doing so he had maintained his family's home, keeping them fed and sheltered during a time of crisis. Few in Cec's position had such an emergency reserve to fall back on. He would have had no regrets doing what he did for the sake of May and the boys.

The new job prompted a move from their house in Barkingside. They rented a house in Meadow Gardens, Edgware, within sight of where he worked. Not long after they moved in, Nanny Woodroffe, who remained devoted to the family, took John and Rees to a Military Tattoo in London where the lads marvelled at the stunt motorcyclists who rode through flaming hoops and made long, spectacular jumps across steep ramps. Boys will be boys – as soon as they got home, they wasted no time setting up their own version of the stunts using some old wooden planks supported on chairs to ride their bicycles over. John soon came a cropper, leading to a visit to Edgware General Hospital for a plaster cast on his broken arm. His parents were not impressed, but at least he had not tried to replicate the leap using flaming hoops.

Cec was determined to set down roots in Edgware, ones that could not be torn up in the next crisis. For many years he had dreamed of owning his own home. His regular income enabled him to obtain a mortgage on a semi-detached house in Stoneyfields Lane, Edgware. It is possible that a substantial amount of the money realised from selling his gold and silver trophies and medals was used to buy the house. Once he had made the decision to start disposing of his collection, it is understandable that Cec may have chosen to continue in order to provide his family with a home. The value of the collection sold was equivalent to at least two years wages, so it must have been a significant sum.

However it was funded, Cecil Griffiths was now a property owner. One of the important documents he retained for the rest of his life was the insurance certificate of the first and only home he ever owned; a combined policy for buildings and contents with the Leeds and Provincial Building Society to the value of £795 with a first annual premium of £1.12s.4d.

The LCS encouraged their large workforce to engage in a wide range of sports organised by the company and their monthly magazine, *The Beehive*, reported on various competitions involving their staff. Their most famous sporting employee was not afraid to take part. Cec reached the semi-finals of the 1932 gentleman's singles tennis competition and his picture was printed in their September issue that year. In March 1933, they featured another photograph of him winning the AAA Championship in 1925 to illustrate an article giving a step-by-step guide to get fit for competition running. Although much of the advice was sound, the dry instructions (recommending plenty of skipping and hopping) hardly enthused the reader.

Cec kept in touch with athletics beyond the pages of *The Beehive*. On 28 August 1937, at London's Motspur Park, he watched Sydney Wooderson break the world record for the mile in the fastest ever time of 4:06.4. Wooderson's coach was Albert Hill, who had broken British records and won Olympic gold medals in Cec's presence. Cec felt exhilarated to be in an athletics stadium once again when a world record was broken. It rekindled memories of the atmosphere at Stamford Bridge in 1926 when he took part in the greatest half mile race in history, sharing in the excitement of Peltzer's world record victory.

Yet after his retirement, Cec's real sporting passion was for football. His team was West Ham United. The years he had spent living in Stratford under the roof of Nanny Wood-roffe had forged his bond with the Hammers, but the First Division status they had enjoyed in the 1920s was long gone and they would languish in the Second Division for the rest of his life.

John and Rees often escorted Cec to home matches at the Boleyn Ground as they grew into teenagers. John failed the scholarship exam and remained in Edgware for his later education. His art skills were recognised by his teachers and he was encouraged to sit an entrance exam for the prestigious Harrow School of Art in 1937. Only 120 pupils went to the school so competition for the forty annual vacancies to start the three-year course was intense, with hundreds applying to be taken on. John was interviewed and examined at length following which he was delighted to be offered a place. He excelled at watercolour painting and was competent with a pencil. The Second World War overtook his studies. Many teachers joined up and the school was closed down, forcing him to leave without a professional qualification.

Rees passed the scholarship exam in 1937 so did not go to the same school as his brother, instead travelling to Orange Hill School in Hendon. There he met his lifelong friend, Ben Beynon, who also shared Welsh roots. They were also alike in looks and had the same gentle temperament – unless they were on the football or cricket field, where their aggressive, skilled play brought them to the attention of local clubs. They were founder members of the Hendon Schoolboys Football Club and played schoolboy soccer in Middlesex. They could have shared the fate of two other boys from the area, Denis and Les Compton, who both played football for Arsenal and cricket for Middlesex, but war broke out in 1939 when Rees and Ben were just fourteen. The long conflict closed many sports clubs for the duration and robbed them of the chance to pursue a career in sport; just like the First World War had done with Cec's rugby. By the time they were released from war service in 1947, their momentum had been lost.

Cec and May also adored their next door neighbours' son, Brian Hex, who was a few years younger than Rees and John. That didn't stop the lads playing football together in their back gardens or on the quiet street in front of the houses. Brian's mother, Jean, was from Pontypridd. She married William Hex in Barnet in 1930.* Brian, who was born in Wales, was their only child.

In the summer holidays of 1938, the two sets of neighbours arranged to go on a two-day trip together to South Wales. Only William owned a car and there was insufficient room for John and Rees, so they were sent on ahead by train to stay with Eva. William was driving, Cec sat on the passenger seat beside him with the excited seven-year-old Brian on his lap, May and Jean sat in the back. The happy holiday mood in the small saloon was shattered when, coming round a sharp bend on the Guildford/Godalming bypass at Milford, a car joining from a spur road struck them on the nearside. The impact wasn't heavy, more of a glancing blow, but William's car overturned and the occupants inside were flung about as it rolled over. Brian was killed instantly.

The inquest, held a week after the crash, was traumatic; both parties blamed each other for the accident. William

---

* It was a joint marriage service – Jean's sister, Jenney, married William's brother, Ernest. It must have been a happy day for both families.

gave his evidence in a distressed state. Cec was distraught when he made his statement, explaining how Brian was sitting between his legs in the front when the other car pulled into them. May and Jean were medically excused from attending because of their injuries – May's head injuries would affect her for the rest of her life – so couldn't comfort their grief-stricken husbands. The other driver, via his solicitor, explained his reason for not seeing the Hex's car as excessive speed on their part, accusing William of travelling at over forty miles per hour. The jury's verdict of death due to misadventure meant the death was caused by an unintentional accident without any violation of law or criminal negligence. No blame was attributed.

The funeral, held at Hendon Park Cemetery, was naturally a sad occasion. A mountain of colourful flowers was placed at the graveside. Very few failed to shed a tear when they saw the wreath with a card attached from Mummy and Daddy. Brian's two little friends handing out wild flowers to relatives as a small tribute wrenched the hearts of the many mourners attending the service.

Cec's sensitive nature made him particularly vulnerable to grief. He felt that he should have been able to protect Brian in the crash. The incident scarred his mind; it was one of the worst chapters in his life. The Griffiths and Hex families spent the next few months under a cloud, constantly aware that Brian was absent. As time passed, the grief subsided and life returned to normal, or as normal as it would get for the next few years. One person was about to throw the life of Cec, and everybody else in Europe, upside-down: Herr Hitler.

Back in military uniform – Cec plays his part
in the Home Guard

17

THE

HOMECOMING

1939-1945

On 20 August 1938, another world record fell to Sydney Wooderson at Motspur Park in a specially-framed half mile handicap. His stunning time of 1:49.2 would have gained Cec's attention and taken his mind away from the grief of Brian Hex's death. Wooderson was the only man on scratch and the inside lane was kept free for him throughout the race, which was actually won by his brother, Stanley, off 85 yards, but Sydney had been specifically timed so the record could be ratified. He was also timed at the 800 metres mark in 1:48.4 to claim that world record also. He held the metric record for eleven months until 15 July 1939, when Rudolph Harbig captured it for Nazi Germany.

War clouds loomed over Europe in the dull summer of 1939 and the nation's mood was darkening. Cec, clearly a natural sportsman, won the annual LCS gentlemen's singles tennis tournament at Osterley Park, but as Nazi Germany captured more than just world records, Cec would return to the grounds of Osterley Park when it was transformed into a military training ground. The racquet in his hand would be replaced by a rifle.

Not content with taking the easy option and watching the progress of the Second World War from the sidelines, Cec became one of the first members of his local Home Guard unit, the 16th Company of the 24th Battalion, Middlesex Regiment, based in Edgware. His reputation as an athlete led to him being assigned the duty of physical fitness training within the battalion; a true challenge considering the age and condition of the recruits. Cec immersed himself in the role.

Cec managed to find employment for John, who had been forced to finish his course at Harrow School of Art early, in the offices of the Woodside Park LCS coal depot. He stayed for a few months until his next job at Elstree Film Studio, where three of his Harrow School of Art colleagues were already working. In 1940, one of John's fellow ex-students who had managed to find work as a commercial draftsman showed him some of his engineering drawings. John was instantly able to interpret the complex principles involved and was invited to visit the firm, BSP Industries Ltd, at their Edgware offices to see how he performed on full-sized drawing boards. They were delighted with the competence of his self-taught technical drawing ability. He put it down to the many years of constructing his Meccano sets.

This fortuitous opportunity encouraged John to resume his education. In order to gain qualifications in his new profession, he attended evening classes at college. At work he was placed in the aeronautical branch of the company. He was assigned to a de Havilland contract concerning the top-secret Mosquito, a radical twin-engine fighter bomber made of wood which became one of the most iconic aircraft of the Second World War. He was involved with the aerodynamic design of the engine nacelles, utilising the air flow over them to capture engine exhaust gasses for wing de-icing. Soon after his eighteenth birthday, with his conscription call-up imminent, BSP Industries was visited by three stern government men who interrogated each employee about their activities. The twelve men on the de Havilland contract, including John, were assessed to be carrying out essential work vital to the war effort and classified as working in a reserved occupation. The Managing Director of BSP Industries, Ivor Bailey, encouraged those who remained to join the Home Guard. John was assigned to the intelligence unit in central London, taking his place alongside other key workers in the same situation as him.

Passing on messages was dull and his father joked that John had it easy. Cec was out in all weathers. Each evening after finishing work, he guarded key local factories and power stations against sabotage by enemy agents or patrolled the streets of Watford, Edgware and Mill Hill keeping a look out for spies dropped from the air. When the Blitz started in September 1940, his role became more active, watching out for and dealing with incendiary bombs. Combat training was stepped up in anticipation of an invasion. John switched units, initially to anti-aircraft guns on Hampstead Heath, then to his father's battalion protecting the streets of Edgware.

As their training progressed they both became uncharacteristically adept at killing potential enemies with a varied array of weapons, some regular issue, others less so. For peace-loving men it was not a skill they took naturally to. Once they were fully trained up and considered proficient they were issued with efficiency badges to sow on to their uniforms. The red cloth badge, just an inch square, was subtly worn on the left forearm, not parallel to the sleeve but balanced on one corner like a diamond. Cec and John were blessed with the meticulous nature and dextrous fingers of Cec's grandfather Benjamin, the tailor. With great pride they wore badges sporting the neatest stitching in the battalion.

Cec had become a sergeant and was responsible for Mills bomb instruction in addition to his physical fitness training. He brought home boxes of hand grenades, eight per box, to remove the heavy protecting grease and prepare them for use. May was none too pleased at having the bombs laid out on the kitchen table. Cec's quick reflexes, honed from years waiting for the starter's pistol, certainly saved lives when one of his men fumbled with a live grenade and dropped it in the throwing pit after pulling out the pin during a training session. The bomb had a seven-second fuse. As men dived for cover, Cec threw himself headlong to grab it and lobbed it over the protecting blast wall just before it exploded. Why he didn't receive at least a citation for his bravery is a mystery; of the 137 medals awarded to members of the Home Guard for brave conduct, 25 involved accidents with live hand grenades. Three were received posthumously.

Accidents on duty and under training caused the deaths of more than 1,600 Home Guard volunteers. A combination of inadequate training on increasingly sophisticated weapons resulted in them facing ever-increasing danger, either at their own hands or at the hands of others. A colleague of Cec was killed instantly during rifle practice when he raised his head from the protective observation pit near the targets to assess the accuracy of the marksmen whom he thought had finished shooting. Cec was always keen to acquaint himself with the weapons he might find himself using if German soldiers came to Edgware. He could strip down and reassemble a Bren gun in rapid time. His competitive streak and nimble fingers ensured that he beat all comers in challenges. Should those Germans arrive, they would also find he was a fine marksman, a common characteristic in top sportsmen.

The war was bad news for Cec's brother, Ben. He lost his prestigious job as a manager of the branch of Austin Reed on the Queen Mary cruise liner when the ship was commandeered for war service as a troopship. His plight was made worse when he was bombed out of his Plymouth home. Ben, his wife Lillian and daughter Margaret were safe in an air raid shelter, but they were now homeless and came to stay at Stoneyfields Lane while waiting for the tenants in their

Brixton home to move out. The house was quite busy for a while and the women became quite fed up with only having two topics of conversation: war or sport. Ben was not only a competent tennis player but a crown green bowling champion, he became the President of the London Welsh Bowling Association after the war.

Cec's duties as a physical training instructor for the Home Guard gave him access to the assault course at the Police Training College in Hendon. He took great delight in putting his men over, under and through the obstacles. His natural speed and athleticism, honed by regular practice, made him nearly unbeatable; Cec often enjoyed humiliating particularly cocky soldiers. He would give them a good start on the course and then romp past them with the grace of a gymnast as they clumsily tried to keep ahead of him. He would then wait for them at the finish, perfectly composed by the time they arrived.

Yet he was not invincible. One evening, after a rigorous session putting his men through their paces on the course, he came home feeling unwell. Although he was grey and short of breath, he didn't admit to having any pain. Cec reassured May that he had just overdone it a bit at the end of a hard day at work.

In 1942 he started a new job with the Navy, Army and Air Force Institutes as a sports manager at the Royal Arsenal in Woolwich, which meant a longer journey on the tube to get to work.

As Rees grew old enough to leave school and become eligible for armed duty, he joined the Royal Air Force Voluntary Reserve. He also found love, meeting Dora Burge while working as a junior clerk at Barclays Bank. As the war slowly turned in favour of the Allies, the RAFVR discharged Rees as surplus to requirements. With the enthusiasm of a young man desperate to make his mark on the war, Rees volunteered for the Royal Welch Fusiliers.

Soon afterwards, Dora fell seriously ill with tuberculosis. Her parents nursed her at home for three months, but she deteriorated and was not expected to live. She was moved to a sanatorium just before Rees was due to commence his training in Wales. The two teenagers in love, unsure of what lay ahead, became engaged. Rees departed for the Brecon Beacons, but the Griffiths family did not abandon Dora. Cec visited her regularly, hoping that she would recover to become his daughter-in-law, but the visits must have brought back painful memories of his own father's death from the terrible disease.

On 3 March 1945, Cec and John travelled the short distance to Tottenham to support West Ham in a wartime London league fixture. They were part of a crowd of over 20,000 which saw their side go down 4-0. One of the goals was scored by Ron Burgess, a Welsh international, which really rubbed salt into the wound. Things took a far worse turn on the return journey. Cec became unconscious in the seat on the train, turning blue in the face. John was given quite a fright, but his father came to and managed to reach home with a bit of assistance. Cec blamed it on the excitement of the football, making a quip or two about the West Ham performance, and explained once again that he had been overdoing it a bit. Long days at the NAAFI, with next to no time off, combined with Home Guard duties at night and what remained of his weekends, made sleep a precious commodity.

He took it easy for a while, experimenting with water-colour painting and listening to Beethoven's string quartets. Both pastimes were the passions of his eldest son. John's artistic talent had been nurtured at the Harrow School of Art; locomotives were his favourite subjects to paint thanks to Lord Burghley's present for his sixth birthday in 1929.

Cec was enjoying spending time with John but worried about the fate of Rees. His youngest son had completed military training and was due home on leave before his regiment left for India. On 6 April, Cec sent him a parcel with the following letter:

Dear Old Cec [Rees].

Just a few lines in with the parcel, which I don't suppose you will get until Monday now, but I don't suppose you do too badly for "grub" over the weekend, so the cakes will come in handy for early in the week and they'll better for keeping a day or two. Do you give some to your pals? And what do they think of them? Do they all get parcels like you? I expect there are some who don't, some who's people can't afford it perhaps.

We are all glad to hear you are having some sport, and are anxious to hear how you got on in the "Rugby sevens", don't forget to let us know all about it. I expect you are as fit as a fiddle now and do not get the aches and pains you used to get after your week-end games home here, except of course for the bruises. We are all eagerly awaiting your home-coming. John hopes you are not going to spend <u>all</u> your time with Dora, he is anticipating taking you out one night. Isn't the news about Dora good? We are all so glad to know she is progressing so wonderfully well and that soon she will be quite all right again.

Well! The war is still hanging on a bit longer, but all the portents indicate that it cannot last a great deal longer, but perhaps after all, my "June forecast" will be about right, and now that the Russians have terminated their agreement with the Japs, perhaps it will not be long before they turn it in too and then everything will be fine. Is Lt. Brown still your Sports Officer? I did some repairs for him some time ago.

Isn't it possible for you to leave Brecon in time to catch the 6:40 from Cardiff on Friday night? I'm sure if you asked your C.O. and told him where you have to go to they'd let you off an hour or so I bet. I should have a try if I were you.

In any case let me know when you expect to arrive at Paddington and I will come to meet you. Do you have to bring all your kit home? Anyway I'll come to meet you.

I am enclosing 70 fags in the parcel 40 of them are from Mrs Butters and the rest from me and Mum. I hope it is enough, you never say do you? Do you get any fags from anyone else?

We have not had any doodles for a week now, so everybody is having some rest.

Well Old Son! I must close now, and will write again soon, don't forget to let me know the time you expect to arrive at Paddington. Mrs Butters sends her kindest regards and John and Mum send their best love and kisses as also does Your Very Loving Dad. XXXXXXXX

On Wednesday 11 April, Cec had a cheerful breakfast with May and set off to work as usual at 7.45 am. He was in a particularly good mood in anticipation of seeing Rees at the weekend after such a long absence. Just 45 minutes later, John answered a telephone call from Edgware General Hospital. His father had collapsed at Edgware Station and was dead on arrival at the hospital. His body was being taken to Hendon Mortuary and needed formal identification. With hardly a pause to register the dreadful news, John set off on this grim task, leaving his mother at home distraught and in a state of shock. Before doing so, he phoned a message to Rees' training unit requesting his immediate release on leave, knowing the devastating effect it would have on his brother.

The post-mortem, carried out the next day, recorded the cause of death as 'aortic incompetence'. For the athlete who had run his races with the heart of a lion it was a perverse judgement.

The family doctor revealed Cec had been diagnosed with a heart condition more than six years earlier and that was the reason why he had not joined the armed services in the fight against Hitler. There was nothing medical that could have been done for him; he had simply been advised to take life easy. It was a measure of Cec's generous character that he did not tell his family. He did not want to burden them with the worry.

Cec was an athlete. He loved to compete and to test himself. He had joined the Home Guard, where he was pushed just as strenuously as if he had been on active service. He did not flinch from the physical training, the weapons instruction, the assault course. The periods where he was unwell after the assault course and on the train had clearly been unheeded warnings of an imminent heart attack. His determination and endurance to keep going afterwards was reminiscent of the superhuman efforts which carried him across the finishing line, often against the odds, ahead of the likes of Edgar Mountain and Douglas Lowe.

On 16 April, a hearse with full attendance collected his body from Hendon Mortuary and transported it to Hendon

Crematorium. A saloon landaulette conveyed his ashes to St Lawrence's Church in Edgware for interment, two additional landaulettes carried the family. It would appear no expense was spared – the cremation shell was sumptuous and the invoice for the service was £45. The grieving widow and her sons may have overstretched slightly since the bill was not paid until 14 August.

The service was attended by many of his friends representing every aspect of his past. Colleagues from the LCS, NAAFI and his Home Guard unit were there to pay him respect, all distressed by his tragic early death. Nanny Woodroffe had outlived him and was there to support the family. His best friend, Jack Gillis, was the only representative from the world of athletics.

The prayer which Cec had copied into the family Bible after his confirmation in 1914 contained the words, 'to judge bothe the quicke and the dead, we maye ryse to the lyfe immortal.' They were prophetic words considering his future success as a runner. How fitting it would have been for the whole of Thomas Cranmer's prayer to have been read from Cec's own writing in that Bible at the service.

Cec's own father had died aged just 47, only two years older than him. Ominously Benjamin's death certificate had incorrectly recorded his age of death as 45; it was correct for his son. Statistics were closely associated with Cec's life. He achieved more than anybody could ever have predicted, but one of those statistical predictions was chillingly accurate. When he was born in 1900, the average life expectancy for a male in the United Kingdom was 45 years.

After the funeral service, May, John, and Rees went home and retrieved Cec's small box of remaining medals. Cec had not allowed them to open the box after he had sold the valuable ones to the pawnbroker, not wishing to be reminded of his loss. Now they wanted to be reminded of *their* loss.

They bemoaned that so many of his prizes had gone. One by one, they opened the presentation boxes to marvel at the treasures they contained. Two boxes were bigger than the rest. Rees flipped open the lid of one to reveal his father's dull Olympic competitor's medal. Although a beautifully crafted object, it was made of bronze and wouldn't have appealed to the pawnbroker who bought the medals.

When he opened the other box, he found a gleaming medal, securely contained in a moulded, velvet-lined, leather display case:

Anvers MCMXX. 1600 Meters Relay * U.K * 1st * C. Griffiths & (G.M. Butler, J.C.A. Davis, R.A. Lindsay.)

Cec's Olympic gold medal stared back at them. They thought it had been sold with all the others. Tears made it impossible for them to look at it for several moments. Then they each held it tightly in turn, mesmerised.

Whether Cec had not sold the medal because, being made predominately of silver, the offer had been too low or whether it was just too important for him to give up, we shall never know. But saving it allowed it to become tangible proof of the most glorious chapter in his life, carrying his priceless legacy forward for generations.

Less than a month after Cec died, the war in Europe ended, just as he had predicted in his last letter to Rees. His Home Guard unit, part of the 24th Battalion, Middlesex Regiment, was chosen to represent the regiment in a military parade to mark all the branches of the armed services which had taken part in the conflict. It was with great pride and deep sorrow that John, with the red efficiency badge sewn on his sleeve, took part in the ceremony. The streets of London were lined with cheering crowds waving flags and banners in celebration of a great victory. Very few noticed the tears streaming down John's cheeks as he thought of his father.

Precious memories – a postcard from the 1920 Olympics
featuring Cec (back row, second from left) and the
successful 4x440 relay squad, including the reserves

18

GONE BUT NOT FORGOTTEN
1945-

Without Cec's income, May was forced to get a job, but she only earned ten shillings a week at a children's clothes shop. The post-war austerity years were difficult and it was only John's income which kept them going. May always cursed the athletics authorities, who she thought regarded Cec as a lower or second-class athlete because of his background and never forgave them for treating her husband so unfairly. Conversely, she enjoyed the high social circles she and Cec had moved in, thriving on her memories in old age, and she often talked with pride of their friendship with Lord Burghley.

The head injuries she suffered in the 1938 car crash always troubled her and may have instigated the mental degeneration she suffered towards the end of her life. She died in 1978 and her ashes were reunited with her beloved husband's at St Lawrence's Church in Edgware.

Between 1948 and 1950, John played football for London Welsh on the right wing, the same position his father had occupied on the rugby field for Neath Schoolboys. He became prolific in the creation of magnificent watercolours, many of them steam locomotives which adorned his house, but sadly were mostly lost when he moved home in 2008. Professionally he reached the highest levels at BSP Industries, building upon the experience he gained with them in the war. He was married in Swansea in May 1951 to Lynne Prosser and moved out of Stoneyfields Lane. They continued to live in the Watford area and had two girls, Caroline in 1954 and Louise in 1964. Their marriage did not last and they divorced in 1974, upon which John moved to his ancestral homeland, Neath, although he also lived in other areas of the country for periods. In 1986 Neath RFC were due to play the New Zealand All Blacks and because of the clash in colours a competition was held to design a shirt for Neath to wear in the match. John won.

John is 91 as this is written. He lives in the confines of a hospital room, unaware of current events and his surroundings, but still responsive to questions concerning his father and reactive to discussion about him.

After the Second World War ended, Rees continued to serve in India. He emulated his father by competing in many sports for his regiment and won a cap for the Welsh military, representing his country in a football tournament for servicemen stationed overseas. That would have made his father extremely proud as he always harboured a hint of regret that his own rugby career had been curtailed so early in his life, perhaps preventing him from receiving the same honour. Rees also rose to the rank of sergeant, the same as Cec in the Home Guard. When he returned home in 1947, two years after being forced to leave Dora in the sanatorium as she fought for her life, they resumed their romance.

His brother John thought he was distant and cold, but what he didn't understand was the mental distress Rees had been put under, leaving his family at the critical time of his father's death and then being separated from them for two years. His health, physically and mentally, had deteriorated. The sporting ambitions he had prior to the war came to nought, but he still played cricket and football for Middlesex clubs.

Rees and Dora married in June 1951, going to live with May at Stoneyfields Lane just a month after John had married Lynn and moved out. Two months after they moved in, *The Times* carried a report, which Rees proudly retained, announcing that Cec's Welsh record for the 440 yards set in 1921 had finally been beaten in a match at Newport by F.P. Higgins. Rees and Dora had a very happy marriage which was blessed with two children; Vanessa in 1954 and Nicholas in 1962.

Rees, like his father, was prone to spasmodic depression. A demanding job with Customs and Excise required him to lead the police on potentially dangerous raids but he was a gentle man and the impending threat of violence would make him physically sick for days as plans for the raids were assembled. The stress caused a nervous breakdown when Vanessa and Nicholas were young – the same age as he and John when Cec plunged into the pit of despair after losing his job during the Great Depression. It was ironic that Rees' depression was due to his work and Cec's by the lack of it.

Rees suffered a massive heart attack in 1984 at the age of 59 but survived to enjoy over ten years of fulfilled retirement with Dora, during which time all of his three granddaughters were born. He did not survive the next heart attack in 1995, dying too young, but at least he lived 24 precious years longer than his father.

Family history has shed some light on the reason for Cec's death. In the last letter Cec wrote before he died, to Rees at his training camp in Wales, Cec referred to the bruising and pain experienced by Rees after participating in sport. Rees' daughter Vanessa suffers the same bruising and pain after exercise, but to an even greater extent. A series of operations on her shoulders and knees following severe dislocations blighted her tennis career and impacted drastically on her active life. In 1990, she was diagnosed with a rare syndrome called Ehlers Danlos which affects connective tissue around the joints and major organs. Its symptoms include easy bruising and hyper-flexible joints. It is a hereditary disease and one of its most serious effects is the weakening of heart muscles which may lead to cardiac arrest. Both Cec and Rees had weak hearts which ultimately killed them, and Rees bruised easily as does Vanessa. It is a good bet that Cec's heart was weakened as a result of Ehlers Danlos.

I married Vanessa in 1978 and we had three girls; Lucy, Beth and Emily. They will be the only descendants of Cec to proudly carry his legacy forwards as his other grandchildren; Caroline, Louise and Nicholas, did not have any children of their own.

Vanessa's mother and Rees' wife, Dora, is still alive, 87 years young. She lives with us in her own annexe, very sound in mind but failing in body as once again she fights a disease, this time the cancer invading her body.

John and Rees fell out and they had had no contact in the ten years preceding Rees's death. The absence of John at his brother's funeral in 1995 was heartfelt by all the family. It was not until I approached John in 2012 for his blessing and help with this book that relationships were gradually restored. Establishing his father's story has mended the broken bridges in the Griffiths family. I hope that is this book's greatest legacy.

*

Robert Lindsay, the athlete who Cec handed the baton to after running the first leg of the 4x400 metres relay in the 1920 Olympics, remained a staunch supporter of Blackheath Harriers after his active days and he always attended club events. After his death in Battersea on 21 October 1958, aged 68, his wife presented the Lindsay Salver, awarded annually to the member whose example and performance in track or field most contributes to the credit of the club.

Jack Ainsworth-Davis, the third-leg runner and surprise package of the 1920 Olympics, retired from athletics in 1921. He became a urological surgeon and was Secretary of the Royal Society of Medicine, establishing a lucrative practice which he gave up to head the surgical division of the hospital at RAF Cosford during the Second World War. There is an unsubstantiated report that he served his country in a more clandestine and military role at this time as a special agent directly recruited by Winston Churchill. He died in Stockland, Devon on 3 January 1976 at the age of 80.

The running career of the all-important anchor leg runner, Guy Butler, paralleled Cec's. He also began competing after the war and retired from athletics in 1929. He became a teacher, then an athletics journalist, during which time he was a pioneer of new training techniques including filming athletes in action. He died in St Neots in Cambridgeshire, on 22 February 1981, aged 81.

Another gold medallist at the 1920 Olympics, Albert Hill, retired from competitive running in 1921. The mild, wet winter of 1924/25 finally dampened Albert's enthusiasm for living in Great Britain. His employment with the railway company left him feeling less than satisfied and attempts to make a full-time career of coaching athletics were making no headway. It must have been with some trepidation when, on 28 January 1925, he boarded the liner *George Washington* with his wife and two young daughters to embark on a new life in Ohio, USA. The horrendously rough Atlantic crossing didn't bode well.

On 7 August 1926, the *Leviathan* docked at Southampton to bring the family home. Albert's dream of starting a new life in the USA had turned into a nightmare. Athletics coaching was equally hard to break into on the western side of the Atlantic. His health had deteriorated; he had lost weight doing heavy manual work in a climate he was not used to. He made the decision to return home with his wife and two daughters, but it meant another new start with a home and job to find. Sadly, Albert's struggles over the past years had forced him to sell nearly all of his medals and trophies. Cec was not the only working-class athlete who was forced to make such a distressing choice by poverty.

It is likely one of Albert and Cec's rivals in the 880 yards, Edgar Mountain, knew of Albert's emigration difficulties when he, his wife and their eighteen-month-old son boarded *City of Genoa* at London Docks on 23 December 1926 to set sail for Cape Town, South Africa. Maybe his fellow Achilles member, Bevil Rudd, had regaled him with great stories about his homeland. Mountain settled in his new country to become Emeritus Professor of Geology at Rhodes University specialising in South African geological formations and discovered several new minerals, one of which, Mountainite, bears his name. He died on 30 April 1985, aged 84, in Grahamstown, South Africa.

Albert Hill at last found full-time coaching employment after the death of Sam Mussabini in 1927, taking over from him at Polytechnic Harriers as well as coaching several other athletics and football clubs. After the Second World War, Albert and his family emigrated again, despite his failed attempt to start a new life in the USA. He died in Ontario in 1969, aged 79.

Jack Gillis also stayed involved in athletics after retirement, becoming a well-known starter, performing that duty at the 1948 Olympic Games in London. He continued to act as a starter almost up to the day he died in 1978, aged 83, in Ferndown, Dorset. Gillis married Rose Thompson, one of the first competitors in women's athletics, in 1931 at West Ham. Cec would surely have been in the congregation to celebrate the marriage of one of his closest friends.

Harold Abrahams' running career may have been ended by injury in 1925, but unlike Cec, he remained part of the athletics scene. He was captain of the British Olympic team in 1928 and became an athletics journalist, working as a commentator for the BBC for fifty years. After defeating Cec in the 1929 election to the AAA, Abrahams worked his way up the ranks, acting as stand-in Secretary on several occasions and eventually becoming President in 1976. He died on 14 January 1978, aged 78.

Eric Liddell ran for the last time in Great Britain on 27 June 1925 at the Scottish Amateur Championship. He won three titles in the 100, 220 and 440 yards and helped the Edinburgh University AC mile medley relay team to victory in his very last race, the same day that Cec attempted the 1,000 metres world record at Stamford Bridge. Liddell then travelled to China to continue with what he regarded as his life's calling, missionary work on behalf of the church.

The Second World War interrupted his mission and he was interned by the Japanese in China. He died from an inoperable brain tumour on 21 February 1945, just five weeks before liberation and seven weeks before Cec's death. Conditions in the camp and a lack of medical treatment may have hastened his death. In 2008, just before the Beijing Olympics, Chinese authorities revealed that Liddell had refused an opportunity to leave the camp, giving up his place for a pregnant woman.

Otto Peltzer, who beat Cec to break the 880 yards and 800 metres world records in 1926, achieved his ambition of representing Germany at the Olympic Games. However, he was left disappointed. He fractured his foot in a handball accident at the mountain school where he taught in the lead up to the 1928 Olympics. Not fully fit, he struggled through the heats but did not qualify for the final. In the 1932 Olympics, where he was team captain, poor organisation led to the German athletes wearing long spikes on a hard track. Struggling with this disadvantage, Peltzer qualified for the final but did not take home a medal.

Peltzer's homosexuality brought him into conflict with the German authorities. Unsurprisingly, he did not represent Germany in the 1936 Olympics in Berlin, which were used as a propaganda weapon by the Nazi regime. He was imprisoned on three occasions, in 1935, 1937 and 1941, ultimately ending up in Mauthausen-Gusen concentration camp. Against all odds he survived the war.

Among the influential friends who campaigned to secure his release from the prison camps was Douglas Lowe, who was the fortuitous beneficiary of Peltzer's injury at the 1928 Olympic Games and won the 800 metres gold medal.

Lowe retired at the end of the year of his second Olympic title, one year ahead of Cec, to become a lawyer. He became

Honorary Secretary of the AAA, succeeding Harry Barclay in 1931 (Barclay died in 1933), a post he held until 1938. He became a judge in 1964 and died in 1981, aged 78, in Cranbrook, Kent.

Gaston Féry was the French 400 metres champion on six occasions, five of which were consecutive titles between 1919 and 1923. He participated in the creation of the Meudon Sports Association in 1937, becoming a player-coach for their football club. He was two months younger than Cec but lived far longer, dying in 1985, aged 85, in Paimpol, France. Féry was remembered as one who lived without worries for the next day. No wonder he and Cec got along so well.

On the same day in 1926 that Cec pursued John Rinkel in the Inter-County Championship relay, it was fitting that Paavo Nurmi, in Stockholm, gained a world record in the 4x1500 metres relay. It was just one of Nurmi's twelve world records ratified by the IAAF at the time, for every distance from 1,500 metres to the marathon, and there were a further twenty unratified records. He would go on to set another ten. Aside from his three gold medals at the 1920 Olympics, Nurmi won five in 1924 and one in 1928. Every time Nurmi notched up another success, Cec would have reflected on what he had written on the postcard in 1920, predicting that Nurmi would 'achieve great things'.

Three days before his first event at the 1932 Olympics, Nurmi was suspended by the IAAF. German race promoters insisted that Nurmi had accepted between $250 and $500 to race in their country the previous year. Although he was never officially declared to be a professional, his suspension was not lifted. He retired in 1934 and moved into coaching and business. As a sign of Finnish affection for their national hero, he was chosen to light the Olympic Flame at the opening ceremony of the 1952 Olympics in Helsinki.

*

Shortly after Cec's death, John contacted Joe Binks at the *News of the World*. Binks had played a crucial role in Cec's success. He had helped Cec find a place in the military running event at Southfields, a crucial stepping stone to getting Cec noticed outside of his native Neath. Ever since then, Binks had been one of Cec's greatest admirers. He wrote a glowing and moving obituary for Cec in his column, mentioning how they first met and chronicled his many successes. It was very long.

Binks was sure that Cec had earned a small place in athletic history, putting forward that idea as soon as Cec hung up his spikes. In the *News of the World* athletics review of 1930, Binks laid into the 'Dismal Jimmies' who delighted in criticising the performance of modern athletes compared to those of old. Things were pretty good, Binks thought. He was in a reflective mood and, perhaps fuelled by Christmas spirit, commented that the 100,000 British athletes in 1,000 clubs affiliated to the AAA had never had it so good. One explanation he offered for the high standard was that Oxbridge athletes were no longer deserting the sport immediately after their studies, thanks in part to the formation of Achilles Club which catered for their needs.

Binks boldly declared, 'That old-time bugbear in sport, "class distinction", has been thoroughly stamped out.' He reflected on the treatment he had received from the arrogant officials when he was starting out on his career. As a junior he often had his race entries returned in favour of better known athletes or because his club, Wandle Harriers, were looked down upon – 'not class enough' – by those in more established circles. The only way to be accepted into some competitions was by personal introduction from a member of the promoting club. As a result of this prejudice and snobbery, he decided not to join a senior club.

Although entirely sincere, he may not have been entirely accurate in his assumption that he was speaking for others when he announced:

> We old timers can thoroughly appreciate what a grand thing it is for the sport to see the Burghleys, Lowes, Butlers and Stallards rubbing shoulders as one happy International team with Cyril Ellis, Cecil Griffiths, Ernest Harper and Harry Payne, to mention only four famous athletes who have come from the mines and the workshops.

As for the athletes of old being better than the athletes of the present day, Binks thought modern runners like Cec were just as good:

> After writing about the high class athletes of the past, it makes one wonder if the present-day men are better. However, we have only to mention A.G. Hill, Cecil Griffiths, H.B. Stallard, C. Ellis and Douglas Lowe to realise that we can still produce wonderful performers.

Cyril Ellis took over Cec's half mile mantle, just as Cec had done in 1922 when Albert Hill departed; the clerk, the miner, and the railway worker all did themselves and their humble origins proud by taking on the might of the establishment with success and dignity.

However, to say that class distinction had been thoroughly stamped out was perhaps taking it too far. Binks had conveniently white-washed across Cec's international ban, only referring to it in vague, general terms. Perhaps Cec's own meek acceptance of the ban helped those within the sport forget about it and not examine the reasons why the AAA had singled him out. Whatever the case, the AAA would continue to pursue any whiff of professionalism with the determination of a bloodhound.

The case of John Tarrant made headlines more than three decades after Cec received his ban. Tarrant's tragic story proved there had been no shift in attitudes at the AAA when it came to a breach of the amateur code by accepting prize money, regardless of the amount, the circumstances involved or the integrity of the recipient.

Cec and Tarrant's stories are chillingly similar. As juniors they both accepted a small amount of prize money from sport, each naive of the consequences. Tarrant took £17 for eight punishing boxing matches which didn't even cover his bus fares to the bouts; Cec took perhaps half that amount for running at charity carnivals. For both of them, the scale of injustice beggars belief.

Tarrant's training for the boxing ring included road running. He was good at it, and he enjoyed it. Realising he would never make the grade as a boxer, Tarrant switched to athletics. He honestly declared his past earnings from boxing when completing the application form to join Salford Harriers in 1952. That was his downfall. A two-year battle with the AAA to be accepted as an amateur was ultimately lost. Tarrant's response to the intransigence of the AAA was to gatecrash prestigious events, running unofficially and numberless, denied refreshment and recognition from the organisers in the results.

With a flavour of drama and theatre, Tarrant would sneak into events wearing a disguise, arriving on the pillion of a motorbike driven by his brother. When the starter's pistol sounded, he would throw aside his loose coat and leap across the barriers, cheered by the crowd and pursued by irate officials who had no chance of catching him. Tarrant accumulated a great deal of support from his fellow competitors and the press, who labelled him the Ghost Runner – like a ghost, there was never any record of his presence on the official result sheets. The AAA eventually relented and he enjoyed two years running officially as an amateur, classified as a reinstated professional. Tarrant was blissfully ignorant that he could not compete internationally and was barred from the 1960 Rome Olympics.

Tarrant was a big, strong man who ran with an ungainly gait. Cec was compact with an elegant style. Yet they were similar in one key regard – they were both fast. Both had the potential to win in the vest of their country at an international level, each was deprived of the opportunity. Their bans were imposed and enforced by officials, invariably privileged, who looked down on and distrusted working-class athletes, especially when money was at stake. Some of the most senior officials who were responsible for preventing the sport being corrupted by money displayed an astonishing level of hypocrisy in their own lives.

While Cec laboured under his international ban, athletes from more privileged backgrounds who were part of the Oxford University, Cambridge University and Achilles athletic clubs were able to continue competing, even if their activities crossed the grey border between professionalism and amateurism.

It is the example of Harold Abrahams that jars hardest in the Cecil Griffiths story. Harold Abrahams was able to employ his professional coach and remain part of the amateur set up, even if his coach was barred entry. Cec's cruel international ban relegated him to the lower ranks of domestic competition and he missed out on widespread acclaim by his exclusion from the 1924 Olympics in Paris. Two of the athletes who won gold medals there, Abrahams and Eric Liddell, were given a form of immortality when their stories were told in the 1981 blockbuster film *Chariots of Fire*. Their subsequent fame has gone on to monopolise the history of their bygone era. Cec was a contemporary of Abrahams and Liddell, but because he was not given the chance to compete alongside them in Paris, his importance in Welsh and British athletics history has mostly been overlooked and his achievements slipped under the radar.

Chariots of Fire was historically inaccurate in several areas for dramatic effect. For this reason, Cec's close friend Lord Burghley refused to associate his name with the script, so he was portrayed by the fictional character Lord Lindsay. Burghley's training using matchboxes on his hurdles was the inspiration behind the film scene where Lindsay clears hurdles with a full champagne glass precariously balanced on them. Burghley's lap of the Great Court at Trinity College is similarly achieved by Lindsay in the film, but he is narrowly beaten by Harold Abrahams. In reality, Abrahams never attempted the challenge. The film also exaggerates the anti-Semitism displayed towards Harold Abrahams at Cambridge.

In addition, the famous scene where Eric Liddell trips in a race and picks himself up to win is depicted at a Scotland v France contest, but it actually occurred when Liddell tripped over Jack Gillis' legs at the 1923 Triangular International. Liddell is then shown finding out about the 100 metres heats being run on a Sunday as he boarded the boat to France for the 1924 Olympics. In reality, he had known for months and had trained specifically for the 400 metres. Nor did a teammate graciously withdraw and offer up a 400 metres place to him as in shown in the film; it was Lancelot Royle in the 200 metres who gave a place which allowed Liddell to win a bronze medal in that event. Moreover, Liddell's sister supported his athletics career. The film portrays her objecting to it.

There are many more inaccuracies. Cecil Griffiths' story needs no embellishment.

Cec was a career athlete who held a full-time job throughout his eleven years of top-level competition; every medal he won or record he broke was earned through hard work and dedication. Many of his contemporaries were only briefly on the athletics scene on their way to a career in the professions, as was the case with Edgar Mountain and Jack Ainsworth-Davis. They came and went, clearly talented but equally privileged to be parachuted into such a position where they were immediately part of the most established and successful athletics clubs in the country, courtesy only of their class and education. Ainsworth-Davis in particular won an Olympic gold medal and little else during his short athletics career while he studied at Cambridge University, the right man in the right place at the right time.

Cec's long-standing records have inevitably been eclipsed and consigned to the past. Athletes have benefited from improvements in track construction, equipment, techniques, health, diet and, ironically, professionalism, which now allows athletes to concentrate full time on their careers.

However, it took a long time after his death for his records to be broken – his Welsh records in the 440 yards and 880 yards fell in 1951 and 1934, while the Welsh all-time bests at the same distances lasted even longer – they eventually toppled in 1953 and 1959. His achievement of winning double Welsh Championship titles in these events three times was never repeated, let alone consecutively, up to when they went metric in 1969 or since. All in all, Cec won ten Welsh Championship titles and held one British and four Welsh records, but if today's criteria for record breaking had applied then he would have accrued an additional four British and six Welsh records.

Cec's performances in the prestigious half mile at Fallowfield, the 1,000 metres at Stockholm in 1924 and the 1,000 metres at Stamford Bridge in 1925 would all have been true British records if the modern criteria for establishing such a standard had been applied then. Instead, they are recognised by historians as the best known performances by British athletes at the time. The other British record which appears not to have been ratified was the 660 yards set at Paddington in 1922.

Cec's 4x440 yards relay British record, set in the 1920 British Empire v USA meeting, stood for four years until a team including Eric Liddell and Guy Butler beat it at the same meeting in 1924. If Cec's ban had not prevented him from being in that team, the margin by which the record was broken would probably have been even greater – Cec was still one of the top 440 yards runners and relay specialists in the country.

He was the AAA Champion at 880 yards in 1923 and 1925. He competed at the AAA Championship – the biggest and most prestigious of all British meetings, effectively the British Championship – for ten consecutive years, always in the top three until he was spiked in 1928. During his career, the only British athlete to run the 880 yards faster was Douglas Lowe, the double Olympic champion of 1924 and 1928.

He won eight titles at the Essex Championships, three at the AAA Southern Championships, five Kinnaird Trophies, countless relays and dozens of individual races ranging from assaults on records at Stamford Bridge to local events on minor tracks. He was regarded as a hero to the large crowds who came to watch him.

Cec's ten years of consistency and effort at the top of British athletics earned him great acclaim, but the ban prevented him from realising his full potential. Cec was a special person subjected to a wrong decision. He would not have been human if he failed to look back with some regrets and wondered how it might have been if circumstances had been different. Yet his character enabled him to overcome the injustice which blighted his career and stifled his rise to the highest echelons of fame and recognition in international athletics. His ultimate destiny was stolen from him, but his talent was beyond the reach of the thieves who governed his sport.

The tragedy of Cec's early death and deprivation of additional international success is compounded by the hardships he suffered in the 1930s, forcing him to sell his medals and trophies. Several items contained a quantity of gold and silver, nearly all were sacrificed on the altar of his family's survival. He only kept one silver and one bronze of his nine AAA Championship medals. Equally disappointing is that all but one of his Welsh Championship medals went the same way. Of approximately a hundred silver cups, trays and cutlery sets he won, not a single item is known to exist. The only remaining trophy is a pewter tray from his 1924 foray in Sweden; its low intrinsic value accounting for its survival. It is most likely everything sold was melted down, but this is by no means certain. Of the few that remained, some of his cups were known to be in the possession of Eva and disposed of by her son.

*

In 2001, when professionalism was finally recognised and accepted by the athletics authorities, the IAAF changed its name from the International Amateur Athletic Federation to the International Association of Athletics Federations. They had literally abandoned the amateurism which they had fiercely protected for more than a century. The AAA remains the Amateur Athletic Association.

In May 2012, Cec was inducted to The Welsh Sports Hall of Fame. In October of the same year, he was the first to receive the same accolade posthumously from Welsh Athletics in their Hall of Fame. Cec now shares a podium with the greatest Welsh sportsmen and women who have ever lived. He is recognised as one of Wales' greatest athletes. But he could have been even greater.

Cec pictured with some of his many trophies.

PHOTOGRAPHS

The 1923 Kinnaird Trophy – Cec breaks the tape first in a close finish; the first four in the 440 yards were separated by two metres.

8. A GOOD FINISH IN THE 440 YARDS.—RIFLEMAN C.
GRIFFITHS (ARMY) BEATS CPL. J. L. MASON (NEW ZEALAND)
ON THE TAPE IN 51 1-5SEC.

The first notable scalp – Cec beats Dan Mason in 1918.

Cec and his wartime trophies.

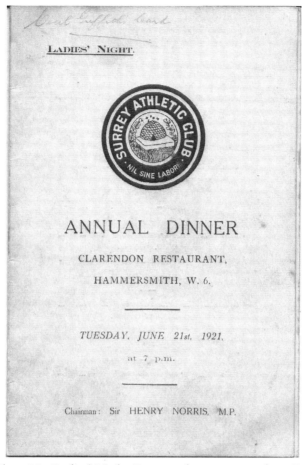

The 1921 Ladies' Night Dinner, the occasion when Cec formed a close friendship with Jack Gillis. The menu shows Surrey AC's beehive emblem (signifying endeavour) with its motto Nil Sine Labore – nothing without labour – an apt motto for Cec's own career with the club of which he was made a life member.

David Feldman Auctioneers

The 1920 Olympics:
Medallist's diploma and competitor's medal (opposite),
participant's lapel pin and Victoire statuette for individual
winners (above), Cec's pinched Olympic flag (below).

WHO WOULD WIN? — E. D. Mountain, the Cambridge student, and C. Griffiths (right), who have had a remarkable series of running successes. A contest has been suggested between them.

Above: The Untouchables – the relay team of Gillis, Royle, Griffiths and Graves at Birmingham in 1923.

Left: Head to head – Cec and Mountain.

PHOTOGRAPHS

Memorabilia saved by Cec: vest badges, Union Jacks, relay
baton, French vest, remaining medals and his father's naval
insignia.

277

Gold medal:
Graham Budd Auctioneers

The AAA Championships:
Gold, silver and bronze medals – the gold belonged to Bert
MacDonald for winning the 1925 one mile title, both of Cec's
were sold to the pawnbroker – and the results of the 1923 AAA
Championship showing Cec in good company.

GREAT SCOTTISH ATHLETE.

Blewitt's Conversion From a Sprinter to a Stayer.

Event	Winners.	Country.	Winner's time or distance.	World's record.	Best in championship.
100 yards	E H Liddell	Scotland	9 7-16sec	9 3-5sec	9 3-10sec‡
220 yards	E H Liddell	Scotland	21 3-5sec	21 1-5sec	21 1-5sec
440 yards	W E Stevenson	England	49 3-5sec	47sec	48⅖sec
880 yards	C R Griffiths	Wales	1min 56 3-5sec	1min 52 1-5sec	1m 54 2-5sec
1 mile	H B Stallard	England	4min 21 3-5sec	4min 12 3-5sec	4m 13 4-5sec
4 miles	C E Blewitt	England	19min 56 3-5sec	19m 23 2-5sec	19min 32sec
1 mile relay	Surrey A C	England	3min 36 4-5sec	—	3m 31 3-5sec
120 y'ds hurdle	F R Gaby	England	15 1-5sec	14 2-5sec	15 1-5sec‡
440 y'ds hurdle	L H Phillips	England	58sec	54 1-5sec	55 2-5sec
2 miles 'chase	P Hodge	England	11min 13 3-5sec	—	10m 57 1-5sec
2 miles walk	G H Watts	England	14min 22sec	13m 11 2-5sec	13min 50sec
Long jump	H M Abrahams	England	23ft 8½in	24ft 11½in	23ft 9½in
High jump	P Lewden	France	6ft	6ft 7 5-16in	6ft 4in†
Pole jump	P Lewden (w.o.)	France	—	13ft 5in	12ft 11in
Putt'g the w'ght	J. Barratt	Ireland	39ft 2½in	51ft 10½in	47ft 4½in
Throw'g javelin	J. Dalrymple	England	148ft 9½in	216ft 9 6-10in	205ft*
Throw'g ham'er	M G Nokes	England	161ft 4½in	189ft 6½in	165ft 8in
Throwi'g discus	G T Mitchell	England	110ft 3in	156ft 1 3-8in	144ft 8½in
Hop, step, jump	J Odde	England	46ft 4½in	50ft 11in	46ft 6½in
Harvey Cup	E H Liddell	Scotland	—	—	—

‡ New championship record created this year.
† After winning championship with 6ft.

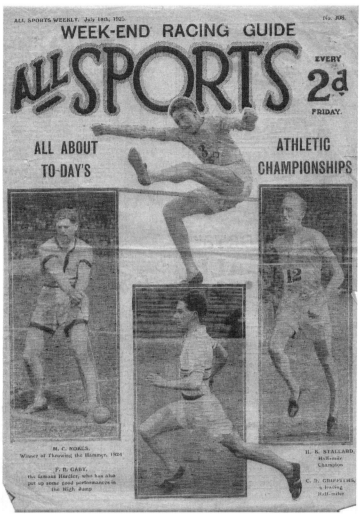

All Sports Weekly depict Cec's long stride and elegant style.
Stallard is described as "the half-mile champion" – by the end
of the day, the new AAA Champion would be Cec.

CECIL GRIFFITHS' DOUBLE AT CARDIFF.

WELSH CHAMPIONSHIP MEETING.

Under ideal conditions, the 12th Welsh amateur championships meeting was brought off on the Cardiff Arms Park, Cardiff football ground, on Saturday. The attendance was disappointing—no doubt due to the sparse way in which the function was advertised.

As anticipated, Cecil Griffiths had no difficulty in accounting for both the 440 yards and 880 yards events, the Surrey A.C. runner being in no way extended.

The final of the 100 yards provided a surprise winner in W. Owens, of Port Talbot, who in the first heat could only run second to Rowe Harding (the holder). In the final, however, Owens ran in determined fashion, and always leading the field won by a couple of inches.

Owens had a successful afternoon, as besides the sprint championship he carried off the 100 yards open.

Another surprise was provided in the two

C. R. GRIFFITHS.

J.B.M.

miles walk, where the holder, W. H. L. Owens, the old Herne Hill Harrier, was well beaten by G. E. Eaton, of Cwmavon. Rowe Harding made amends for losing the 100 yards title by gaining the 220 yards event, after a terrific struggle with Venables, the Cardiff Rugby footballer.

The mile event produced one of the best races of the afternoon, and Richards well deserved his success in beating such an experienced runner as E. Thomas. The latter, however, had no difficulty in winning the four miles event, and thus regained the honour which he lost to Edwards last year.

WINNER OF MANY CUPS.

Rifleman Cecil Griffiths, Queen's Westminster Rifles, of Neath, is already a proved champion on the running track, although he is but 18 years of age. Returning home on leave, he brought with him many trophies won in international and brigade sports. His latest success was at Stamford Bridge on Saturday, when he achieved distinction by winning the quarter-mile against picked representatives of the British Army, Navy, and Air Force, America, New Zealand, Canada, and Australia. Rifleman Griffiths is the son of the late Councillor Ben Griffiths and of Mrs Griffiths, Agincourt House, Neath, and brother of Mr Ben Griffiths, a well-known Neath business man. He is in training at Wimbledon.

Rfn. C. Griffiths.

SOUTH WALES TIDE TABLE.
(From Brown's Nautical Almanac.)

Cec in the press: 1918 (above), 1923 (left) and 1926 (below).

WORLD'S RECORD
GERMAN WINS GREATEST HALF MILE IN HISTORY.
Lowe Also Inside Meredith's Figures: London Beaten In The Sprint Final.—By Olympus.

The best runner Wales has produced: Cec's second-place medal from the 1927 Welsh Championship and *All Sports Weekly*'s judgement from 1924.

The author and his wife, proudly declaring their ancestry at the 2012 Olympics

ACKNOWLEDGEMENTS

It was the two sons of Cecil Griffiths, Rees and John, who provided the spark to launch me on a journey of discovery about their father's life which would take me two intense years to complete.

I met Rees in 1972, shortly after embarking on my life-long romance with his daughter Vanessa, who I married in 1978. Vanessa and I attended different schools in Dunstable, but like Cec and May in 1915 and Benjamin and Sarah in the 1880s, sport helped to bring us together. Early in our relationship, I learned that her grandfather had won an Olympic gold medal. One day, Rees retrieved it from the loft to show me. I will never forget the awe I experienced the first time I held that iconic emblem of achievement in sport, which was probably the reason why the story about the man who won it only half registered in my brain.

Rees did not talk much about his father's treatment at the hands of those who administered athletics, but I realised it was an emotional issue when I found out he would never watch *Chariots of Fire*. That film, for him, represented the tragedy of his father's life, only paying homage to the upper-class, elite university athletes who lived in a different world to the one occupied by his father. Rees was cast from the same mould as Cec. He was a dignified and much-loved man, respected by all and loved by many, but he went to his grave in 1995 still harbouring resentment that history had not been kind to his father. I missed my chance to learn much more about Cec's fascinating story. That is how the situation remained until early in 2012, when I decided to do something about it.

Unfortunately, at that time all I knew was his name and the basics of his Olympic odyssey from some of his memorabilia, a few photographs and the story of his death. We had no contemporary press cuttings, only a *Daily Telegraph* article about him written during the 2004 Olympics. There were precious few medals and trophies. Only two people remembered him; one was his eldest son John, aged 89. The other was his daughter-in-law Dora, Rees' wife and my mother-in-law, just a few years younger than John. They both carried precious information passed down through the family which could not have been obtained from any other source. A unique legacy treasured by Vanessa is that she is the only member of the family born at the house in Stoney-fields Lane, Edgware which was partly paid for by the medals her grandfather sold.

My first task was to search the internet but every website I discovered provided little additional information to what I already knew about him and without exception contained incorrect information about his birth and death which clearly emanated from a common source – the respected author Ian Buchanan's *Who's Who of UK and GB International Athletes 1896-1939*, the definitive reference book on the subject. Apart from those discrepancies, this book provided key information about Cec's career highlights.

John and Rees grew up very close, but as is the wont with families, the brothers fell out following the death of their mother in 1978. The situation was not retrieved by the time of Rees' death in 1995. John exiled himself in Neath, the birthplace of his father, and resisted all contact with his brother's family until I tentatively wrote to him in 2012 asking about his father. He replied answering most of my questions and following an exchange of letters we met and formed a strong friendship. His memories, which had been locked away for many years, flooded forth, bringing him great joy and providing me with a rich vein of personal information and research material.

When I first met John he was independent, in possession of his faculties and living in a house similar to the one his father had been born in only a few roads away. Exactly coinciding with the point in time when he had exhausted his memories of his father, John's physical and mental health deteriorated. Following a series of falls at home, he was admitted into hospital in November 2013; he is unlikely to leave. It was as though he had been hanging on to his father's story and, once he had placed it into my care, he gave up on life.

My sincere thanks go to John's next-door neighbours, Robert and Christine, who have done so much for him, as has his friend Gareth. Their efforts enabled him to live as long as possible in his precious home, surrounded by memories of his father, as his health failed. The hospitality and local knowledge provided by Robert and Christine on my frequent visits to Neath was much appreciated and enhanced my efforts to immerse myself in the town's geography and history.

Another local man who played a key role in understanding Cec's family's involvement with their local church, St David's, was Canon Stephen Ryan, Rector of Neath. Immediately following my approach to him about Cec he enthusiastically announced in the Neath Parish magazine that their town had produced a successful Olympian and a book about him was in the pipeline. I hope they are pleased with the result.

Another reverend Welshman, Arthur Morris from Sketty, was instrumental in bringing Cec to the attention of the Welsh Sports Hall of Fame in 2002 and making me realise that Wales would want to know Cec's story. Sadly he passed away in 2009 and is greatly missed by his family who I know will take comfort from his wish being fulfilled.

The discovery of *The History of Welsh Athletics*, co-written by Clive Williams, was a revelation. It provided a wealth of statistics and personal information about Cec. It was Clive's efforts that resulted in Cec being inducted into the Welsh

Sports Hall of Fame and the Welsh Athletics Hall of Fame in 2012. The help and advice that Clive has given me, a first-time author, has been instrumental in driving this book forwards. At stages when my research hit a wall, an email to him always produced a rapid response with the answer or the contact details of another expert who might be able to help me.

Thanks to Clive I have been assisted by several eminent authors and historians. Early in my quest, Mel Watman was able to expand upon the statistics in Ian Buchanan's book and put me in touch with the family of Jack Gillis, who was Cec's teammate and best friend.

Ian Deaves, the nephew of Jack, is a prominent athletics official, along with his wife Susan. The information Ian gave me about Jack was unavailable elsewhere. There is precious little about him on the internet, despite his clash with Eric Liddell in 1923 which provided for a dramatic scene in *Chariots of Fire*.

Peter Lovesey, who doubles his career as a crime writer with being an athletics historian, and Kevin Kelly, the Herne Hill Harriers' historian, have provided an immense contribution, explaining many confusing and often intriguing aspects of Cec's career. Peter's explanation of the changing nature of the different types of British records was the blueprint for the language used to simplify this complex subject in this biography. I was deeply moved by Peter's admission that when he wrote his first book in 1967 he had communicated directly with two significant characters associated with Cec; Douglas Lowe and Henry Stallard. In the rare event of Peter not being able to answer a question, his extensive contacts within the world of athletics would save the day. Kevin helped reveal Cec's impressive record between 1922 and 1928 in the Kinnaird Trophy, records which had proved impossible for me to discover.

Bob Phillips, editor of *Track Stats*, and his colleague Rooney Magnusson solved the mystery about Cec's trip to Sweden. Bob's input regarding the relaxed attitude towards record breaking and the necessary criteria to achieve records during the 1920s was fundamental to understanding why some were ratified and others forgotten. Peter Matthews, editor of *The International Track and Field Annual* supplied the British All-Time Best lists for 880 yards and 1,000 metres, both of which include Cec. Keith Morbey, an expert on relays, was able to assist in answering key questions about the 4x400 metres race at the 1920 Olympics.

I have read many books, but I should single out for praise *The Ghost Runner* by Bill Jones. Its exploration of John Tarrant's ban for professionalism by the AAA ominously echoes the story of Cec. I also made great use of Matthew Llewellyn's essay, 'Olympic Games Are an International Farce – The 1920 Antwerp Games and the Question of Great Britain's Participation', published in *Olympika: The International Journal of Olympic Studies*.

I owe a debt to the staff at several libraries. Claire Smith at Neath Reference Library and David Morris at West Glamorgan Archive Services were on the spot to search for scarce education records and other information appertaining to Cec and his family. I am not only grateful for what they found but also for their expertise in knowing where to look for data which proved not to have been retained, as that saved me a lot of fruitless research. To Claire and her colleagues, I appreciate the cheerful and patient help you gave me as I waded through the microfiche copies of over 1,500 local newspapers to successfully locate one half of my Holy Grail – the race in which Cec competed as a youth, central to his later ban, only previously alluded to in the history books. It was my first 'eureka' moment in the project. In fact, I found three races, the precise one which the authorities latched on to is unknown.

I thank the ladies at Pontardawe Library who were generous with their time in helping me solve the riddle woven by Cec himself, about where he actually competed in the pivotal races. It was they who put me in touch with the local historian and author, Keri Thomas, Vice-Chair of the Swansea Valley History Society, whose detailed description of past and present athletics tracks in Pontardawe was instrumental in identifying the location where Cec would have run during the First World War.

Harriet Eaton, the Heritage Education Officer at Neath Library, proved an outstanding ally to discover more about Cec's family, especially William Trick and his alleged misconduct during the First World War. The many hours of research she carried out on my behalf certainly went beyond the call of duty. In her role as Secretary to the Neath Port Talbot Heritage Group, the introduction she gave me to local historian, Jeff Childs, resulted in him providing me with expert advice on potential sources of information about Cec's early races. My first serendipitous meeting with Harriet resulted in many enjoyable hours together examining the library records and her interest in Cec knew no bounds. Her email message, 'it was a pleasure meeting and working with you,' is a source of great personal pride. It was the first time I had worked alongside anybody since a car accident in 2005.

Joanne McCloskey, who works in the Heritage Department of Belfast Central Library, certainly saved me a visit to Northern Ireland in order to determine whether Cec raced there in the Triangular International Contest of 1921. The information she sent me from the *Belfast News Letter* about that weekend was breathtaking. Similarly Katie Ormerod, at St Bartholomew's Hospital Archives and Museum solved the riddle of Cec's apparent involvement in the 1926 inter-hospitals race.

I am also in debt to the professional archivists at the University of Birmingham in charge of the Amateur Athletic Association papers held in the Cadbury Research Library, who worked tirelessly to help me in my less-than-successful look for the other half of my ultimate objective – the information the AAA acted upon in 1923 to administer Cec's ban. Ivana Frian was another to go above the call of duty in answering my follow-up questions, which I am sure required her to conduct her own research. To Vickie, Ian, Anne and all of the others who showed such great interest in my quest, I am very grateful.

Confirmation of the circumstances which resulted in Cec's ban and who orchestrated it has probably been lost to history. In view of the International Amateur Athletic Federation's direct involvement in Paavo Nurmi's suspension in 1932, I was concerned that they may have been the prime movers regarding Cec. Imre Matrahazi, Technical Manager of the IAAF's Competition Department, researched their documents and sent me the minutes of their Congresses for 1923 and 1924. There is no mention of Cecil Griffiths in any of their existing papers of that period which somewhat rules them out of the equation. My thanks go to Imre. All evidence suggests it was the AAA responding to the IAAF's 1923 resolution on amateur status but there is no audit trail to prove this or any mention of it in the comprehensive minutes of their various committees which I have scrutinised.

For some time I knew that I had insufficient knowledge about Cec to attempt anything like his biography so I thought laterally about how to chronicle his history and add interest in another area. One of Cec's teammates at the 1920 Olympics was Albert Hill, with whom he had an encounter on the eve of an important day in the Olympic stadium for both of them. Their similar working-class backgrounds divided them from the elite upper-class athletes who dominated athletics during the 1920s, so it seemed appropriate to write a book combining their exciting and interesting lives. To this end I contacted Tony Mason, the Emeritus Professor of History at De Montfort University, who specialises in the relationship between sports and the military in Britain. He provided me with a considerable amount of information about Hill's life which proved incredibly useful.

Andrew Cormack and Peter Devitt at the RAF Museum in Hendon welcomed me beyond my expectations, providing me with all I needed and much more about Hill's service with the Royal Flying Corps. The jewel in their crown was the photograph album of the 1920 Olympic Games held in their archives in which I was amazed to find images of Cec and the British team. I will never forget how my nerves churned when Andrew placed that album on the table in front of me and casually observed my vandalistic attempts to prize apart the leaves of the book which hadn't been opened for many decades.

At this point I knew nothing about Cec's early life, not even which school he went to, but Carole Marriot provided the breakthrough I needed to write Cec's biography. Carole had married Eva's grandson, Nicholas, Cec's great-nephew. Fortunately, she had kept in contact with Dora. Following Sarah's death, Eva became the custodian of the family's documents, photographs and many of Cec's trophies; her children, Honor (Nicholas' mother) and William, eventually assumed these responsibilities. William did not marry and continued to live in Eva's Porthcawl house until he died in 1986, leaving it in such a neglected state that Carole and Nicholas feared entering in case they transferred any infection to their young son, Chris, who was in hospital with leukaemia. They recovered what they could, including the priceless family Bible with inscriptions showing the births and deaths of Cec's siblings, but much had deteriorated beyond salvation or been lost. The silverware was also missing, presumably disposed of by William.

Nicholas died in 2000 but Carole kept the documents, realising the importance of them to Chris, who survived his illness, and his sister Emma; they are the only living descendants of Eva. My visit to Carole was the breakthrough I needed; it was a second 'eureka' moment which would drive me forward. It is difficult to single out the most important discovery in her collection, but the letters from Sarah to Eva explaining the hopeless financial state Cec was in after losing his job were fundamental to understanding why he sold his medals.

There have been a number of other people who have embraced my efforts to produce this biography. Individuals such as David Thurlow, Sydney Wooderson's biographer, and Paul Willcox, the historian for Achilles Club, were able to provide long forgotten information about Achilles athletes. Roger Counter, Vice-President of Blackheath Harriers, was perfectly placed to furnish details about Robert Lindsay after he retired from active athletics. For the discovery on French websites of Gaston Féry's post-athletics history, I must thank our daughter Lucy, a French teacher.

Lucy, like her great-great-grandmother, Sarah Trick, has married a patriotic Welshman with a passion for sport. Her husband, Rhodri Humphreys, who swam for Wales as a junior, is also a Royal Navy Officer, sharing Benjamin Griffiths' background, and is one of their elite swimmers. If Lucy and Rhodri are blessed with children perhaps history will continue to repeat itself with another sporting champion, maybe the next Welsh Olympic gold medallist. Our other daughters also remind us of their origins. Beth has the auburn, Celtic colouring of Rees; Emily the porcelain complexion of May.

An unexpected source of knowledge was via RootsChat. com in the shape of their anonymous contributor, hanes teulu, an Aristocrat of the Family History Forum. In a series of exchanged messages, he/she from Swansea, provided me with valuable local history and prevented me going off on a tangent when searching for the location of the races at 'Pontardawe and around there'. It was a very satisfying encounter from an area of the internet I have not previously experienced.

Ironically, it was Rees who provided a late impetus to his father's biography. It had been a cause of concern that so few tangible records had been kept about Cec's achievements. I should have known better. Despite Dora's insistence that she held nothing relevant, I decided to search once more through the vast amount of bags and boxes transferred to our house when she moved in with us in 2000. In a plastic carrier bag which I had previously missed, I found dozens of press cuttings and photographs which rendered me in a state of unbridled euphoria for hours as I skimmed through them. Rees had not let me down.

I wish I had more intimate knowledge and understanding of Cec. There is little for me to link with him other than the opinions of others, mainly journalists and ex-athletes, and the fading memories of John and Dora. Trying to get inside Cec's mind to understand what made him tick has been like trying to conduct a forensic autopsy without a body. I regret that the words probably, perhaps, and possibly occur all too frequently in this biography.

The precise number of races Cec competed in is unknown, but he was a prolific competitor and won many awards. He was good at what he did because he did it a lot, and he did it a lot because he was good at it. In just two months spanning his marriage in 1922, he ran in fifteen races at ten different meetings throughout England, Wales and Scotland. Perhaps he competed at two hundred meetings during his career – if so I have discovered the details of less than half of those, so not in any way does this biography represent a comprehensive account of his involvement in athletics. I have only included the ones which had a bearing on his career or how they affected him personally.

For any errors of fact which professional historians and expert athletics enthusiasts may identify, I apologise. I have diligently attempted to verify all the material I have incorporated but invariably some will say, 'that's not right.'

Hopefully Cec's biography will regenerate interest in him and bring him to the attention of the Welsh nation. It is my intention to encourage the Neath and Port Talbot Council to recognise him in a variety of ways. A memorial or a road named after him would be appropriate, but I would like to take that one stage further. I intend to launch a campaign to establish his favourite canal walk from Neath to Aberdulais as a nationally-recognised circular route officially bearing his name. It is spectacularly scenic, has facilities at the halfway point and is accessible to all.

The ashes of Cec and May are buried at St Lawrence's Church in Edgware in an unmarked grave. His family could not afford a headstone at the time and surprisingly it has never been attended to. Plans are underway to provide an engraved stone gloriously recognising the Welsh Olympian who won gold and was laid to rest far from the country which he loved.

In July 1972, the AAA held a dinner in the Strangers' Dining Room at the House of Commons to bring fifteen British Olympic gold medal winners together under one roof for a nostalgic celebration, including Cec's relay teammates. Rees must have painfully regretted his father's absence as he kept the *Daily Express* report of the function. The picture they carried featured many of the characters in this book; David Jacobs, Lord Burghley (by then the Marquess of Exeter), Douglas Lowe, Guy Butler, Harold Abrahams, Jack Ainsworth-Davis and Lynn Davies.

The Olympics in 2020 would provide a sensational centenary backdrop to bring together the gold medals won by Cec, Guy Butler, Jack Ainsworth-Davis and Robert Lindsay in Antwerp. It would provide a boost for our Olympic involvement in Tokyo, so let's make this reunion a reality. Please get in touch if you can help.

I thank Scott at Chequered Flag Publishing for the vision he had in taking Cec's biography on and the belief he had in me. I certainly felt by time he had led me through the demanding process to produce this book it had become our project. It was extremely rewarding to hone the story with somebody else who had a knowledge of its content equal to mine but a clearer vision of the way forward.

Nearly finally, a caveat is necessary to anybody contemplating writing their first book. Be prepared for your whole being to be ruled by your subject for a considerable period of time. Every other aspect of your life will suffer and your loved ones will become frustrated with your lack of concentration on necessary family routine. My thanks to Vanessa for allowing me some slack while writing this. I apologise wholeheartedly for the God-given and oft-used excuse for neglecting some duty or another: 'it is about your grandfather!'

Finally, thanks to the BBC and Eddie Butler, who won sixteen rugby caps for Wales between 1980 and 1982. He presented a BBC2 Wales programme in July 2012, *A Play-*

ground for the Posh, in which he examined whether the early Olympics were only open for the upper classes. To this end he and a film crew visited us to discover the story behind Cecil Griffiths, the working-class athlete from Neath who indeed managed to play on the playground for the posh in 1920 at Antwerp. It was with great delight and pride that we welcomed Eddie into our home to hear first-hand his superlative rich voice and witness his consummate professionalism in the making of the programme. He had a genuine interest in Cec, particularly his involvement with Neath Schoolboys. As he examined Cec's memorabilia and held Cec's Olympic gold medal, he made a profound statement which I will always revere:

'He won an Olympic gold medal and played rugby for Neath. How could life get any better?'

John Hanna
jchanna@hotmail.co.uk

STATISTICS

<u>Olympic track and field medallists from Wales</u>

Games	Name	Event	Medal
1912 Stockholm	David Jacobs	4x100m Relay	Gold
1920 Antwerp	**Cecil Griffiths**	**4x400m Relay**	**Gold**
1920 Antwerp	Jack Ainsworth-Davis	4x400m Relay	Gold
1948 London	Ken Jones	4x100m Relay	Silver
1948 London	Tom Richards	Marathon	Silver
1952 Helsinki	John Disley	3000m Steeplechase	Bronze
1960 Rome	Nick Whitehead	4x100m Relay	Bronze
1964 Tokyo	Lynn Davies	Long Jump	Gold
1980 Moscow	Michelle Probert-Scutt	4x400m Relay	Bronze
1988 Seoul	Colin Jackson	110m Hurdles	Silver
1996 Atlanta	Jamie Baulch	4x400m Relay	Silver
1996 Atlanta	Iwan Thomas	4x400m Relay	Silver
2004 Athens	Catherine Murphy	4x400m Relay	Bronze

Selected results from AAA Championships 1919-1928

Date	Event	First	Second	Third
5 July 1919	440 yards	Guy Butler	Nils Engdahl (Swe)	**Cecil Griffiths**
2/3 July 1920	440 yards	Bevil Rudd	Guy Butler	**Cecil Griffiths**
1/2 July 1921	440 yards	Robert Lindsay	Bevil Rudd	**Cecil Griffiths**
	Medley relay	Polytechnic Harriers	**Surrey AC (CG 440y)**	Kingston AC
30 June/1 July 1922	880 yards	Edgar Mountain	**Cecil Griffiths**	Paul Martin (Sui)
	Medley relay	**Surrey AC (CG 880y)**	Polytechnic Harriers	S London Harriers
6/7 July 1923	880 yards	**Cecil Griffiths**	Edgar Mountain	Sydney Spencer
20/21 June 1924	880 yards	Henry Stallard	Douglas Lowe	**Cecil Griffiths**
	Medley relay	**Surrey AC (CG 880y)**	London AC	Polytechnic Harriers
17/18 July 1925	880 yards	**Cecil Griffiths**	William Nelson	Ray Dodge (USA)
	Medley relay	Achilles	**Surrey AC (CG 880y)**	Herne Hill Harriers
2/3 July 1926	880 yards	Otto Peltzer (Ger)	Douglas Lowe	**Cecil Griffiths**
1/2 July 1927	880 yards	Douglas Lowe	**Cecil Griffiths**	René Féger (Fra)
	4x440 yards relay	Achilles	**Surrey AC (CG anchor)**	Herne Hill Harriers
6/7 July 1928	880 yards	Douglas Lowe	Hermann Engelhard (Ger)	Wilfred Tatham

Selected results from Welsh Championships 1920-1929

Date	Location	Event	Position (Time)
4 Sept 1920	Newport Athletic Grounds	100 yards 440 yards	Second First (51.4)
16 July 1921	Barry Athletic Club	220 yards 440 yards	First (23.0) First (49.8)
19 Aug 1922	Cardiff Arms Park	440 yards 880 yards	First (54.4) First (1:59.2)
14 July 1923	Cardiff Arms Park	440 yards 880 yards	First (54.0) First 2:07.0
24 May 1924	Newport Athletic Grounds	440 yards 880 yards	First (55.0) First (2:05.8)
17 July 1925	Pontypool Park	Did not compete (clash with AAA)	
2 Aug 1926	Newport Athletic Grounds	Did not compete (reason unknown)	
6 June 1927	Penarth Recreation Ground	440 yards 880 yards	Second First (2:06.4)
16 June 1928	Newport Athletic Ground	Did not compete (reason unknown)	
20 July 1929	Cardiff Arms Park	Did not compete (reason unknown)	

Records broken by Cecil Griffiths

British record: achieved by an athlete of any nation competing in Great Britain.
British best: achieved by a British athlete competing anywhere in the world.
Welsh record: achieved by an athlete of any nation competing in Wales.
Welsh best: achieved by a Welsh athlete competing anywhere in the world
* Record previously/subsequently held by Cecil Griffiths.

Date	Meeting (Location)	Event	Time	Record (Previous/Subsequent)
11 Sept 1920	British Empire Games, Stamford Bridge	4x440 yards	3:20.8 (CG 49.8)	British record (1908/1924)
16 July 1921	Welsh Champs, Barry Island	220 yards	23.0	Welsh record (equal) (1908/1926)
		440 yards	49.8	Welsh record (1914/1951)
				Welsh best (1910/1953)
15 Sept 1921	Paddington	660 yards	1:21.4	British best (1916/?)
10 June 1922	Kinnaird Trophy, Stamford Bridge	880 yards	1:58.0	Welsh best (1906/1922*)
1 July 1922	AAA Champs, Stamford Bridge	880 yards	1:55.8	Welsh best (1922*/1922*)
19 Aug 1922	Welsh Champs, Cardiff Arms Park	880 yards	1:59.2	Welsh record (1906-1923*)
26 Aug 1922	Metropolitan Police Sports, Herne Hill	880 yards	1:55.2	Welsh best (1922*/1924*)
29 July 1923	England v France, Paris	800 metres	1:57.0	Welsh best (first known/1929)
6 Aug 1923	Rodney Parade, Newport	880 yards	1:57.6	Welsh record (1922*/1934)
16 Aug 1924	Fallowfield, Manchester	880 yards	1:54.6 Also identical time at same event in 1925	British best (equal) (1888/1926)
				Welsh best (1922*/1959)
23 Sept 1924	Stockholm	1000 metres	2:33.6	British best (1914/1925*)
27 June 1925	Stamford Bridge	1000 metres	2:31.8	British best (1924*/1927)
3 July 1926	AAA Champs, Stamford Bridge	880 yards	1:53.1 (est)	Welsh best (1924*/1959)

Evolution of British best 880 yards performances 1882-1938 (compiled by Peter Matthews)

1:57.0	Walter George	4 Nov 1882	New York
1:57.0	Francis Cross	26 Feb 1887	Oxford
1:56.8	Francis Cross	24 Nov 1887	Oxford
1:56.4	Francis Cross	7 Mar 1888	Oxford
1:54.6	Francis Cross	9 Mar 1888	Oxford
1:54.6	Herbert Workman	7 Sept 1901	Montreal
1:54.6	Henry Stallard	21 June 1924	Stamford Bridge
1:54.6	**Cecil Griffiths**	**8 Aug 1924**	**Fallowfield**
1:53.4	Douglas Lowe	11 July 1925	Cambridge, USA
1:53.2	Tommy Hampson	5 July 1930	Stamford Bridge
1:52.4	Tommy Hampson	21 Aug 1930	Hamilton
1:52.2	Godfrey Brown	17 July 1937	Princeton
1:50.9	Sydney Wooderson	1 Aug 1938	White City
1:49.2	Sydney Wooderson	20 Aug 1938	Motspur Park

Evolution of British best 1000 metres performances 1905-1949 (compiled by Peter Matthews)

2:46.2	Edwin Montagu	12 June 1905	Paris
2:35.2	Edwin Owen	27 June 1914	Huddersfield
2:33.6	**Cecil Griffiths**	**23 Sept 1924**	**Stockholm**
2:31.8	**Cecil Griffiths**	**27 June 1925**	**Stamford Bridge**
2:27.8	Cyril Ellis	30 July 1927	Fallowfield
2:24.6	Bill Nankeville	17 Sept 1949	Brussels

May and John, Cec's wife and son, in 1923

INDEX

Index

Chequered Flag
PUBLISHING

www.chequeredflagpublishing.co.uk